Children's Rights

Look for these and other books in the Lucent Overview Series:

Abortion
Adoption
Advertising
Alcoholism
Cancer
Child Abuse
Children's Rights
Drug Abuse
Drugs and Sports
Eating Disorders
Euthanasia
Family Violence
Gangs
Gay Rights
Homeless Children
Homelessness
Illegal Immigration
Illiteracy

Juvenile Crime
Mental Illness
Population
Poverty
Prisons
Recycling
Schools
Smoking
Sports in America
Suicide
Teen Alcoholism
Teen Pregnancy
Teen Sexuality
Teen Suicide
Women's Rights
World Hunger

Children's Rights

by Ann Malaspina

LUCENT
BOOKS

LUCENT *Overview Series*

LUCENT *Overview Series*

Library of Congress Cataloging-in-Publication Data

Malaspina, Ann, 1957–
    Children's rights / by Ann Malaspina.
       p. cm. — (Lucent overview series)
    Includes bibliographical references and index.
    Summary: Discusses issues relating to children's rights such
as equal access to education, health care, rights in schools, and
the juvenile justice system.
    ISBN 1-56006-175-8   (alk. paper)
    1. Children's rights—United States—Juvenile literature. 2. Child
welfare—United States—Juvenile literature. 3. Children—Legal
status, laws, etc.—United States—Juvenile literature.   4. Children
—Services for—United States—Juvenile literature.   [1. Children's
rights.] I. Title. II. Series.
HQ789.M34   1998
305.23'0973—dc21   97-35064
                                             CIP
                                             AC

Copyright © 1998 by Lucent Books, Inc.
P.O. Box 289011, San Diego, CA 92198-9011
Printed in the U.S.A.

Contents

Introduction

TODAY'S YOUNG PEOPLE face restrictions on their activities that would have been unimaginable just a few decades ago. Teenagers in a California high school must take an alcohol Breathalyzer test in order to attend their winter prom. The television industry is developing the V-chip, an electronic device to allow parents to selectively block programs, for example, with violent or sexual content. In Georgia, a fifteen-year-old who skips classes risks losing his or her learner's driving permit.

Do these and other restrictions violate the rights of children? In fact, since the 1960s, judges and lawmakers have guaranteed minors many important civil rights, some of which were previously granted only to adults. Disability rights laws promise the first grader who uses a wheelchair the right to attend regular classes in the local public school, while a U.S. Supreme Court decision gave juveniles accused of a crime the right to legal counsel.

Protecting children

The movement toward granting rights to children recognizes that youths are unlike adults but are nonetheless protected by the Bill of Rights, the first ten amendments to the Constitution which guard against unjust and unreasonable actions of government. Children do not have the maturity and experience to make some decisions or to face some serious consequences, but they are still citizens.

Most people agree that children sometimes need special protections. Children under a certain age cannot drive, buy

cigarettes, or drink alcohol. Federal child labor laws exempt minors from dangerous tasks in the workplace, and state child abuse laws shield them from harm in dysfunctional families.

Children today are granted more civil rights than ever before, but they also experience a greater number of restrictions.

Curfews

Yet efforts to protect children and control their behavior can sometimes infringe on their civil liberties. Since the early 1990s, public concern over juvenile crime has led about one thousand cities and towns, and many large retail malls, to impose teen curfews, according to a report by Facts On File News Services. Teen curfews make it illegal for minors to be in public places during certain hours.

In 1996, Dade County, Florida, enacted an 11 P.M. to 6 A.M. curfew for children under age seventeen from Sunday through Thursday, with a midnight curfew on Friday and Saturday. In the first nine months of the curfew, more than sixteen hundred youths were picked up by officers and temporarily detained, Metro-Dade police captain Mark McGrath said.

Proponents of teen curfews say the laws help prevent teenagers from causing trouble or becoming victims of crime, and they assist parents in monitoring their children in the evening. Curfews in Phoenix, Dallas, and New Orleans have been credited for reducing juvenile crime in those cities.

A delicate balance

But civil libertarians protest that curfew laws violate children's right to freedom of assembly as guaranteed by the First Amendment. This fundamental right to gather in public, they say, applies to children as well as adults. Critics charge that such laws unfairly target law-abiding teens and interfere with parents' right to rear their children as they see fit.

Tiana Hutchins, a sixteen-year-old Washington, D.C., resident, was stopped by a police officer for a possible cur-

A sign states a 10 P.M. curfew for people under seventeen. Curfews are seen by some as a means of reducing juvenile crime, while others feel that they violate young people's rights.

few violation while talking with a friend in front of her own home. "It is unfair to punish good kids who are out trying to make something of themselves when only a small percentage of young people are committing crimes in the city during curfew hours," said Hutchins, who was lead plaintiff in a class-action suit challenging the D.C. curfew, filed by the American Civil Liberties Union (ACLU).

But D.C. councilman Harold Brazil, a sponsor of the curfew legislation, defended it in a report by the Freedom Forum First Amendment Center: "We are trying to make our streets safe and make our kids safe, and these folks are splitting hairs."

In 1993, a federal appeals court upheld a Dallas curfew, ruling that it was justified by a compelling state interest in fighting juvenile crime. Three years later, the D.C. curfew law, which was similar to that in effect in Dallas, was struck down by a federal court on constitutional grounds. U.S. District Judge Emmet G. Sullivan said that minors "possess a fundamental right to free movement to participate in legitimate activities that do not adversely impact on the rights of others."

For now, teen curfews continue to be controversial, highlighting the delicate balance between providing children with special protections while respecting and preserving their individual rights and freedom.

1

Equal Access to Education

ALL CHILDREN IN the United States are guaranteed a free public primary and secondary education. The fifty states spell out this important right in their constitutions, which also make school attendance compulsory from first grade until the age of fourteen to eighteen, depending on the state.

By opening their doors to every child, public schools prepare each generation to move on to higher education, enter the workforce, and contribute to society. Public education is considered a great equalizer, vital to a democracy, the means by which youths from many backgrounds are given a similar chance to excel and achieve. Yet some people believe our commitment to public education does not always live up to its promise of equal access for all children. Prior to the 1950s, black children in Arkansas could not sit at school desks alongside whites; as recently as 1986, an Indiana boy with AIDS had to fight a court battle to attend his local middle school. Children with disabilities, even in the 1990s, are struggling for equal opportunities in school.

While primary responsibility for the system of public education lies with the states, federal legislators and the Supreme Court have brought about sweeping changes in education since the 1950s, mandating that states integrate classrooms and respect the rights of disabled students, for example. Both levels of government face continuing questions about providing every child, equally, with the best possible education.

Minority access

Black students have had a long struggle for equal rights in education. When the Supreme Court upheld the principle of separate but equal treatment for the races in *Plessy v. Ferguson* (1896), black children were entitled to a free public education, but in seventeen states and the District of Columbia they were forced to attend segregated schools. All too often black children were educated in ramshackle buildings by underpaid teachers with inferior materials. In 1947, the all-black Robert Moton High School in Farmville, Virginia, was a one-story overcrowded building with a temporary addition constructed of wood and tar paper and heated with stoves. Moton had no gymnasium, no lockers, no cafeteria, substandard toilets, and no auditorium; the science teachers had no equipment to teach classes. The town's white school, Farmville High, had all these facilities, and its teachers were paid more than Moton's, writes Margaret Dornfeld in *The Turning Tide*. In 1950, Moton

A 1941 photo of a segregated school in Georgia shows students crammed together, without desks or a blackboard. Although black children received free public education, they attended inferior schools.

The 1954 Supreme Court decision to desegregate schools was often met with resistance. Here, demonstrators in Little Rock, Arkansas, protest the admittance of black students to their schools.

High students went on strike to protest the poor conditions, but an historic lawsuit brought by the National Association for the Advancement of Colored People (NAACP) in 1952 on behalf of the students, contesting the Virginia law requiring separate schools for blacks and whites, failed in federal court in Richmond.

Still, the student strike at Moton High was a beginning. With the growth of the civil rights movement in the 1960s, more and more people would criticize school segregation laws. For thousands of black children, equal access to education was a promise denied.

"Inherently unequal"

After parents in four states challenged the laws that forced their children to attend inferior schools in 1954, the U.S. Supreme Court in *Brown v. Board of Education of*

Topeka, Kansas, ruled unanimously that school segregation violates the Fourteenth Amendment of the U.S. Constitution, which guarantees all citizens equal protection under the law. The nominal plaintiff was Linda Brown, a black Topeka student prohibited from attending her neighborhood school, Sumner Elementary, which admitted white students only.

Separating children by race generates a sense of inferiority, the justices stated. "We conclude that in the field of public education the doctrine of 'separate but equal' has no place. Separate educational facilities are inherently unequal," wrote Chief Justice Earl Warren in the landmark decision.

With the *Brown* decision, states could no longer separate students by race, but school desegregation did not come easily. In 1957, President Dwight D. Eisenhower sent federal troops to ensure the safety of black students in a previously all-white high school in Little Rock, Arkansas, over the opposition of Governor Orval Faubus, who was determined to keep white and black students apart. In other cities, violence erupted over plans to bus students long distances to achieve integration.

After the Civil Rights Act of 1964 outlawed discrimination in federally funded programs, school districts across the country were forced to integrate or risk losing vital federal dollars. Yet school desegregation created its own problems. Fearing the schools would deteriorate, whites in Boston and other cities with court-ordered busing and other integration programs fled to private schools or the suburbs. By the 1990s, 80 percent of Boston's public school students were nonwhite and some schools in black neighborhoods enrolled no white students at all.

Resegregation

In fact, urban schools across the country have become "largely black and poor . . . because dismal schools have frightened away both the black and white middle class," wrote *New York Times* columnist Brent Staples in May 1997. Schools are becoming resegregated in the 1990s faster than ever, according to Professor Gary Orfield at the Harvard

Graduate School of Education. Thus, the inequities that existed before *Brown* have not disappeared. "We may be deciding to bet the future of the country once more on separate but equal," writes Orfield in a 1997 report, "Deepening Segregation in American Public Schools."

Studies show that racial imbalance in schools is often accompanied by poverty, limited resources, low academic achievement, and more students with special needs. Author Jonathan Kozol traveled the nation to examine the effects of poverty and racial inequality in schools. In his book *Savage Inequalities: Children in America's Schools*, Kozol writes that "segregated schools are inherently unequal . . . because segregation cuts students off from critical paths to success in American society."

Some cities in the 1990s are under pressure to improve educational access for minority students. The Connecticut Supreme Court ruled in 1996 that public schools in Greater Hartford fail to provide students with equal educational opportunity because of segregation by race and ethnicity. The court found that existing school district lines create racial imbalance between inner-city schools, with 95 percent black and Hispanic student populations, and the almost all-white suburban schools. Urban students score significantly lower on standardized tests than students in the suburbs. The state is under a court order to relieve racial imbalance and guarantee educational equality for all Greater Hartford students.

School funding

Along with racial imbalance, school funding policies have been blamed for inequalities in public education. Public schools operate in urban neighborhoods and affluent suburbs alike, but less money is spent on students in poorer communities. While many factors contribute to a good school, without money to pay qualified teachers, buy new books, or fix broken windows, schools will struggle to compete.

Local property taxes contribute nearly half of most school budgets. Because houses in poor neighborhoods are

worth less than houses in wealthy neighborhoods, the amount collected in property taxes (based on property value) in poor neighborhoods is usually much lower than the amount collected in wealthy neighborhoods. So poorer communities have less money for teacher salaries, school building projects, books, and other supplies. Beginning in the late 1960s, parents and educators filed lawsuits challenging school financing policies as discriminatory and asking states to equalize spending in rich and poor districts.

In 1973, the Supreme Court considered a Texas case brought by the father of children who attended an inner-city high school in San Antonio. The Court decided the Texas system of school financing did not violate the Constitution because education was not subject to the federal guarantee of equal protection; school financing was, rather, a matter for state lawmakers to decide.

In some seventeen states, however, the courts decided school financing systems did violate state constitutions, especially when funding differences were excessive. After more than twenty-five years of school finance disputes in New Jersey, in 1997 the New Jersey Supreme Court declared the twenty-eight poorest school districts were inadequately funded in violation of the state constitution's mandate to educate all children. "For many years [the children in those districts] have been denied their constitutional right to a thorough and efficient education," declared the court.

Not everyone agrees that increased school funding is the best way to improve the quality of education. New Jersey governor Christine Todd Whitman opposed increased funding, instead advocating strict academic standards to boost student performance. Some research shows that student achievement is not directly linked to school spending unless the money funds class size reduction, math and science class enrichment, teacher training, or similar programs.

Children with disabilities

Race and economics are not the only factors that affect a child's access to education. Children with disabilities and their parents have fought for years to receive the same educational opportunities as other students.

Until the 1970s, children with special needs were often placed in segregated classes or schools or denied enrollment in public school altogether. Then in 1972, the Pennsylvania Association for Retarded Citizens and the parents of seventeen children with mental retardation won a class action suit challenging a state law that kept children out of school if they were deemed "uneducable and untrainable."

In the spirit of this and other lawsuits brought by parents, Congress passed Public Law 94-142, the Education for All Handicapped Children Act of 1975, later renamed the Individuals with Disabilities Education Act. The law assures the 5.4 million children in the United States with physical and mental disabilities a free, appropriate public education, protects the rights of the children and their parents, and guarantees federal funds to help schools comply. Schools cannot turn a child away because of mental retardation, speech impairment, emotional problems, physical disabilities, learning disabilities, or other special needs.

When President George Bush signed the Americans with Disabilities Act on July 26, 1990, he extended to the dis-

Students with special needs, such as this autistic boy, are placed in regular classrooms whenever possible and are entitled to counseling, rehabilitation, and transportation.

abled population full civil rights protections and equal opportunity in all areas of society, from employment to public transportation. The ADA also ensures equal opportunity in public schools.

Mainstreaming

Today states must provide children with disabilities with a free, appropriate public education, including an assessment of their special needs and an individualized education program describing the services the school will provide. A disabled child must be educated in the least restrictive setting; this means "mainstreaming" the child, or placing him or her in a regular classroom, if possible. The child also has a right to related services such as counseling, rehabilitation, medical services, and transportation, and parents have a right to participate in decisions.

Placing students with disabilities in regular classrooms, however, presents challenges for everyone. Not only must school districts bear the costs of adapting classrooms to accommodate disabled children, but mainstreaming is not the answer for every child. Teachers may not have the training to handle the child's particular needs or the resources to develop multiple instructional plans, or the child may require such a high degree of attention that insufficient attention is given to other students.

Sometimes, school officials and parents unable to agree on what is appropriate for the child turn to the courts, which rely on federal and state disability laws. Mark Hartmann, who is autistic, was removed from his second-grade classroom in Ashburn Elementary School in Loudoun County, Virginia, after school officials decided he would be better off in a class with children with similar disabilities. His parents waged a two-year court battle to return Mark to a regular classroom, where they felt he would receive a better education. Unlike the school officials, they felt Mark could flourish in the class, without causing disruptions. In December 1996, a federal district court judge found that the school's decision to remove Mark from school violated a federal law requiring school districts to make every effort to mainstream children with disabilities, reported the *Washington Post*.

Parents across the country are watching closely to make sure children with disabilities have the same educational opportunities as other children. In cities such as San Diego and Los Angeles, parents in recent years have gone to court to force schools to overhaul special education programs and mainstream more children in regular classrooms. New federal support for their effort came when President Bill Clinton signed a bill in 1997 providing $4 billion to help classroom teachers learn how to educate children with disabilities.

Children with HIV/AIDS

When AIDS, the deadly illness that destroys the body's immune system, first appeared in the United States in the early 1980s, parents and teachers confronted a disability they did not yet understand. People began contracting the human immunodeficiency virus (HIV), which causes

AIDS, before anyone knew how to prevent infection or treat the disease.

Some people felt the best safeguard was to shield themselves from any contact with people who were HIV-positive. As a result, people with AIDS were ousted from their apartments, fired from their jobs, and turned away by their doctors. Laws protecting AIDS patients from discrimination varied from state to state, but no federal antibias law was yet recognized.

Many parents did not want their children to attend school with students infected with HIV. Newspapers reported incidents of young students turned away from day-care centers and public schools. AIDS discrimination in the schools became a national issue with the case of Ryan White, the Indiana teenager who helped change the way people looked at the disease and its victims.

Before his death in 1990, Ryan White participated in class from his home via telephone. The line was hooked up after the Kokomo, Indiana, school board prevented White from attending school.

White contracted the virus from a blood transfusion to treat hemophilia, a genetic disease that prevents the blood from clotting. After he was diagnosed with AIDS in 1984, the school board in Kokomo, Indiana, refused to allow him to attend his local middle school. His mother, Jeanne, filed a discrimination suit and the school decided to allow him back, but a group of parents sued to keep him out. The suit failed, and White reentered school, but he was not welcomed. "When we had to team up in class, no one wanted to be my partner," he wrote in his autobiography, *Ryan White: My Own Story*. He died in 1990.

In 1988 the Supreme Court ruled that an important civil rights law passed in 1973 prohibits discrimination based on fears of a contagious disease, including AIDS. The Americans with Disabilities Act of 1990 also made it illegal to discriminate against people with AIDS. These two federal laws, coupled with laws in some states prohibiting AIDS discrimination, guarantee children with the virus equal access to public schools.

Widely disseminated AIDS education has taught most people that AIDS is not transmitted from one person to another through casual contact, but rather through the exchange of blood, semen, or vaginal excretions. Most schools have policies ensuring that precautions are taken to reduce the risk of transmissions. Teachers keep plastic gloves in their desk drawers in case a child has a cut or nosebleed, and students with open sores are sent home or given a bandage.

As a result, students with HIV or AIDS are more accepted in schools today. "Part of it is the changing attitude on the part of schools and school administrators on how to handle HIV and AIDS. It's become abundantly clear there is no appreciable risk of HIV transmission in a classroom setting," says Frank Baran, managing editor of *AIDS Policy and Law*.

Illegal immigrants

Even some who support all children's right to free public education have questioned whether one group of children —illegal immigrants—should be granted the same right. Responding to a surge in illegal immigration in the early

1990s, some people wanted to discourage new and prospective arrivals by reducing public spending on health, housing, welfare, and education.

Immigrants to the United States enjoy the same constitutional protections against discrimination as any citizen. A landmark 1982 Supreme Court decision assured immigrant children, including the children of people who have entered the United States illegally, a right to a free public elementary and secondary education.

But with illegal immigration soaring—an estimated 3.4 million undocumented aliens lived in the United States in 1992—urban schools in cities like New York and Los Angeles are coping with overcrowded classrooms and thousands of students who are just learning English. The United States spends about $3.1 billion each year educating illegal immigrants, and more for bilingual education, according to a report by the Urban Institute, a public policy research group.

Proposition 187

Looking for ways to stem illegal immigration and save money, in November 1994, California voters approved by 59 percent a ballot initiative, Proposition 187, which would deny most basic services, including public education, to any person who is not a citizen or legal resident. The law would also deny nonemergency health and welfare services to illegal immigrants.

California had roughly 1.6 million unauthorized immigrants in 1994, according to the Immigration and Naturalization Service. "It's time to regain control of our nation's borders and restore integrity to our nation's laws," said California governor Pete Wilson, who favors Proposition 187 and tough restrictions on illegal immigration.

Opponents say the law violates America's commitment to providing all children with a free public education. In a visit to San Francisco before the 1994 election, President Bill Clinton said the proposed law would push more kids onto the streets and "turn the teachers into police officers," according to news reports.

Students in California protest Proposition 187, which would deny public education to illegal immigrants.

This was not the first attempt to bar illegal immigrants from public schools. In 1982, the Supreme Court struck down a Texas law that prevented the children of illegal immigrants from attending public school. In *Plyler v. Doe*, the Court stated that the law violated the federal constitution by denying children education, and in so doing causing irreparable harm.

A year after Proposition 187 was passed, a federal judge declared parts of the law unconstitutional. U.S. district judge Mariana Pfaelzer ruled in 1995 that undocumented aliens cannot be asked their immigration status when applying to attend public schools or for health and welfare benefits because the state would be illegally attempting to control immigration, which is a federal function under the Constitution.

Federal efforts to take similar action also failed. In 1996, Congress debated the Gallegly Amendment, which would allow states to ban illegal immigrant children from public schools, but the proposal was dropped from a larger education bill after protests from children's rights advocates and President Clinton.

For now, the United States has to look for other ways to curb illegal immigration than by turning children away from public school. "Denying education to undocumented children under current law is unconstitutional," says Kathy Imahara, staff attorney at the National Immigration Law Center. "Parents should know that schools are not allowed to ask for Social Security numbers. They can only ask for birth and baptismal records to confirm the child's age, immunization records, and proof the child lives in the school district."

Tuition vouchers

While some people believe tax dollars should not be spent on educating illegal immigrants, others are so fed up with public schools that they want government to pay tuition for private schools. In some communities with troubled school systems, low-income families want the option to send their children to private and parochial schools. These parents, who could not ordinarily afford to pay school tuition, believe their children should have the same access to quality education as children from wealthier families, even if the cost of that equal opportunity is borne by the state's taxpayers.

In 1990, Milwaukee, Wisconsin, was the first school system to offer low-income families tax-free vouchers to pay for private, secular schools. Milwaukee's schools are largely attended by minority students, and the citywide high school graduation rate is just 45 percent, even lower in the poorest neighborhoods. The city's private and parochial schools are more integrated and students both perform better and graduate in higher numbers. About nineteen hundred mostly black and Hispanic students applied for the program in 1996 for vouchers worth about $4,400 each.

Tuition vouchers are part of a national movement to give public school students more choices. About two-thirds of the states have school choice programs, which allow students to attend schools outside their neighborhoods. In Cambridge, Massachusetts, and New York City, students may request the school with a philosophy or curriculum they feel is best for them, even if it is across town.

The voucher controversy

While many choice programs are widely praised, tuition vouchers are controversial. Those who support voucher programs believe that children, rich or poor, have a right to attend the school of their choice, even if it is private. "There are a lot of people who want a good education for their children, and they can't afford it. Vouchers would help them out a lot," LaWanda Womack, a single working parent in Cleveland told the *Cleveland Plain Dealer.* She needed vouchers to help send three of her children to her Catholic parish school.

But critics say that voucher programs remove dollars and motivated students from the public schools, creating new inequities. Some states, including New Jersey, have barred voucher programs because state laws prohibit tax dollars from being spent on nonpublic schools.

A 1996 Phi Delta Kappa/Gallup poll found 61 percent of Americans reject the idea of allowing parents to choose a private school at public expense. "If there's anything we don't need, it's the diversion of public funds to fund the private purse," said Ron Marecw, president of the Ohio Federation of Teachers, in the *Cleveland Plain Dealer*.

The Cleveland voucher program, begun in September 1996, allowed students to use the funds for parochial and religious schools. But in May 1997, a state appeals court ruled the program violated the constitutional separation between church and state by spending tax dollars on religious education. Still, many parents believe their children should have a right to attend the school of their choice, even a school affiliated with a religious denomination.

The growing interest in school choice reflects the crisis in public education today. Plagued by violence, underachievement, and overcrowded classrooms, many inner-city schools are in danger of failing in their mission to help the next generation become educated and productive adults. While the United States has come a long way since 1951, when Linda Brown could not attend her local elementary school because she was black, the goal of educational equity is still elusive for many students.

2

Students' Rights in School

WHILE ALL CHILDREN have the right to attend public school, their individual rights in school are often weighed against the school's mission to provide a safe educational environment for all students. The public school setting creates a set of special circumstances. Unless they are enrolled in private or parochial school or home-schooled, children are required to attend public schools, which are funded by public tax dollars and governed by local, state, and federal laws. Schools, in turn, must fulfill their promise to educate students and keep them safe while they are on school property.

Courts have often sided with school officials in giving higher priority to the education and welfare of all students over the interests of a single student. Thus, a child's constitutional rights may legitimately be waived in the hallways and classrooms.

This clash of interests—a student's rights versus the school's educational mission—has provoked controversies over nearly every aspect of student life, from dress codes to reading lists. Two areas in particular have raised difficult questions about the rights of public school students: the Constitution's guarantee of freedom of expression and the right to privacy.

Freedom of expression

"Congress shall make no law respecting an establishment of religion, or prohibiting the free exercise thereof; or abridging the freedom of speech, or of the press; or the right of this people peaceably to assemble, and to petition the government for a redress of grievances."

The First Amendment of the Bill of Rights establishes the right of Americans to freely express themselves. This important constitutional guarantee, a fundamental feature of our democracy, means that people are free to state their opinions and beliefs. They can say or write what they choose, wear the clothes they like best, and read the books that appeal to them.

Yet students in public schools often discover their right to free expression is not absolute. Sometimes school officials decide that freedom of expression for one person infringes on the rights of others. For example, when five seniors at

The Bill of Rights includes the First Amendment, which guarantees Americans the right to practice religion, express their opinions freely, and assemble peaceably.

Greenwich High School, in Greenwich, Connecticut, secretly inserted a coded message of racial hatred in their 1995 yearbook captions, the principal suspended them, disqualifying them from graduation. The community was outraged by the message of bigotry, and the school paid to reprint the yearbook. In this case, no voices protested that the students' First Amendment rights were violated.

Dress codes

While few would disagree that schools should not allow students to make racist remarks that are harmful and disruptive, sometimes a student's self-expression is not so clearly out of bounds, as in the case of the student who dyes her hair pink or wears a controversial T-shirt.

A student's clothes or hairstyle may be a fundamental form of personal expression, but schools have to weigh this constitutional right with the school's goal to educate and maintain order. This issue surfaced in September 1996 when a gay Burlington (Vermont) High School student was repeatedly sent home for wearing a dress to school. The principal felt the student was disrupting learning.

It arose again in 1996 in Muskogee, Oklahoma. High school seniors signed a statement saying they understood the graduation ceremony dress code, which prohibited ethnic symbols. So when an American Indian hung an eagle feather from her mortarboard and two blacks wore African tribal cloth with their graduation gowns, they were denied their high school diplomas. The same issue surfaced in North Hadley, Massachusetts, in 1993, when a student who wore a T-shirt reading "Coed Naked Band. Do it to the rhythm" to his gym class was told by the teacher he could not wear it to school. After he protested to the local school board, the board passed a strict dress code, prohibiting students from wearing anything the board deemed obscene, lewd, profane, or vulgar.

Many schools have similar dress codes, which may also prohibit clothes which demean others on the basis of race, sex, or religion, or advertise alcohol or illegal drugs. School districts generally establish their own dress codes, which often reflect the standards of the community.

When disputes arise over dress codes, courts have usually decided that local school boards do have the right to regulate student clothing and hairstyles if the regulations are not arbitrary and do serve a purpose, such as preventing violence or gang activity. In general, dress regulations must have some educational purpose and not discriminate unfairly against students because of race, religion, or other factors.

In their book *School Rights*, Tom Condon and Patricia Wolff write that rules that ban immodest clothing or that uphold safety measures are usually acceptable, as are rules against T-shirts with vulgar messages and clothing with gang colors or symbols. "But rules that simply reflect taste—rules against pants for girls, or tie-dyed shirts, or jeans, are sometimes thrown out," they write.

Censorship

Just as students are generally expected to dress in ways that do not disrupt the classroom, students writing for school publications must act responsibly. They cannot print statements that are libelous—that is, false and damaging to a person's reputation—or that invade a person's privacy. They have to follow the copyright law, and refrain from printing obscene or indecent material according to community standards.

But can a student, like any journalist in the United States, publish controversial or provocative articles in the school newspaper? A significant blow to a free student press came in 1988 when the Supreme Court limited the First Amendment protections for student journalists.

In 1983, the principal at Hazelwood East High School in suburban St. Louis, Missouri, censored two articles about teen pregnancy at the high school and the effects of divorce on children in the school newspaper, *Spectrum*, published by a journalism class. The article on teen pregnancy contained personal accounts of three Hazelwood East students who became pregnant. Principal Robert Reynolds decided that the article, which included frank discussions of birth control and sexual activity, was inappropriate for a school newspaper

'EXTRA! EXTRA!.. Read some about it!..'

and student readers and did not protect the girls' anonymity. He objected to the piece on divorce in part because it included an interview with a student who faulted his father for not spending time with the family, but failed to balance the article with an interview with the father.

Reynolds decided to delete the two pages on which the articles appeared. Outraged that their rights as journalists were being curtailed, Cathy Kuhlmeier and two fellow students on the newspaper sued the school for violating their First Amendment rights to free expression.

After two lower court battles in which the litigants took turns suing each other, the Supreme Court decided in *Hazelwood School District v. Kuhlmeier* that the principal acted reasonably and did not violate the students' constitutional rights. "We hold that educators do not offend the First Amendment by exercising editorial control over the style and content of student speech in school-sponsored expressive activities so long as their actions are reasonably related to legitimate pedagogical concerns," wrote Justice Byron White. The high court declared it was "not unreasonable" for the principal to decide discussions on sexual activity and birth control were inappropriate in a school newspaper distributed to fourteen-year-old freshmen.

Hazelwood's message is that a school can sometimes censor student speech that conflicts with its educational mission, even if that speech would not be banned outside of school. The decision was not unanimous: "Such unthinking contempt for individual rights is intolerable from any state official. It is particularly insidious from one to whom the public entrusts the task of inculcating in its youth an appreciation for the cherished democratic liberties that our Constitution guarantees," wrote Justice William Brennan in his dissent, joined by Thurgood Marshall and Harry Blackmun.

Hazelwood significantly curtailed the First Amendment protections provided to students nearly two decades earlier. These safeguards were first spelled out in the landmark 1969 court case *Tinker v. Des Moines Independent Community School District*, in which the justices ruled that students could wear black armbands to school to protest the Vietnam War. At that time, the high court declared schools may limit expression only when it could substantially disrupt student activities or infringe on the rights of others. "It can hardly be argued that either students or teachers shed their constitutional rights to freedom of speech or expression at the schoolhouse gate," stated Justice Abe Fortas.

After *Hazelwood*

Some observers worry the *Hazelwood* decision has hurt high school journalism. "It has had a significant impact in not only giving school authorities more power to influence the school newspaper, but also the yearbook and other expressive activities going on in school, and to have students conform to their conception of what the publications should cover," says Paul McMasters, executive director of the Freedom Forum First Amendment Center at Vanderbilt University in Nashville.

The Freedom Forum reported in a 1994 study of student journalism, *Death By Cheeseburger*, that restrictions on high school newspapers have increased in the past twenty years. In a survey of 270 high school newspaper advisers, 37 percent said school principals had censored articles or required changes due to content. "The long-term effect is very damaging to democracy," says McMasters. "Students who are allowed a wide latitude in expressive activities tend to do better, academically and socially. Those who are restricted or repressed learn that 'might makes right.' They go out ill-equipped to become leaders in the community."

33

Calls to the Student Press Law Center in Virginia, which advises high school and college journalists on censorship issues, have increased 150 percent since 1988, says director Mark Goodman, an attorney. "It's been pretty devastating," he says of *Hazelwood*, noting that many administrators believe the decision gives them free rein to censor indiscriminately when in fact the Court's decision applies only to school-sponsored publications that are not public forums for student expression. Goodman and his staff counsel students on their rights under their school's journalism policy and provide suggestions on discussing First Amendment issues with administrators. Going to court is a last resort.

Investigative articles critical of school policy or school officials and controversial topics, such as drugs, homosexuality, birth control, and AIDS, are most likely to raise objections, says Goodman. At Charles Henderson High School in Troy, Alabama, the student editors of *Trojan Myths* in 1994 were ordered by school officials not to publish a survey finding increased use of drugs among high school sophomores in Alabama, even though two antidrug stories were to accompany the survey. The editors finally printed story headlines over two blank pages in protest, reported *Seventeen* magazine.

Some states, including Massachusetts, Arkansas, California, Colorado, Iowa, and Kansas, have state laws protecting students from undue censorship. In 1997, Illinois legislators passed the Illinois Student Publications Act giving students control over the content of their publications, under faculty supervision, and prohibiting censorship except for libel, obscenity, or speech harmful to minors. "This bill protects against the arbitrary censorship which has flourished in the high school press since Hazelwood," says Nick Samuels, director of the High School Civil Liberties Education Project of the American Civil Liberties Union of Illinois.

Free speech on the Internet

With over half the nation's public schools hooked up to the Internet, the worldwide information library available to anyone with a computer and an access code, the right of students to express themselves and seek information online is under increasing scrutiny. A group of suburban Chicago students told the *Chicago Tribune* they used school computers to browse pornography and learn how to pull off credit card scams, consume and manufacture drugs, and build bombs. But many students use the Internet to research term papers, communicate with friends via e-mail, and explore entirely innocent topics of interest.

Some school officials fear unrestricted use of the Internet could jeopardize school computer programs. In response, schools have installed filtering software to block access to Internet chat rooms and websites considered offensive.

Students in many schools are required to follow Internet Acceptable Use Policies, or AUPs, which ban students from using obscenities, copying software, and using the Internet for illegal activities. At Francisco Bravo Medical Magnet High School in Los Angeles, students study a handbook and take a quiz on the school's Internet rules, and their parents sign permission slips, before they log on. If they violate the rules, they lose their Internet privileges and may even be expelled, reported the *Los Angeles Times*.

A Supreme Court decision

Yet First Amendment advocates caution that Internet restrictions could threaten the free expression rights of students to gather information and communicate ideas. In 1997 the Supreme Court struck down parts of the 1996 Communications Decency Act banning the transmission of all "obscene or indecent" material over the Internet to minors. In *Reno v. ACLU* the Court ruled that "the interest in encouraging freedom of expression in a democratic society outweighs any theoretical but unproven benefit of censorship." The law went too far, the justices decided, by failing to exclude material that could have "serious literary, artistic, political or scientific value" to minors.

The decision was a victory for advocates of unrestricted use of the Internet for minors, although schools are still free to impose Internet use policies. "Only by allowing student reporters open access to information—on the Internet and elsewhere—can we help them develop the skills they need to be critical thinkers and to communicate important information to their teen audiences," commented Candace Perkins Bowen, former president of the Journalism Education Association, in a report by the Student Press Law Center.

School safety

Like the right to free speech, a student's right to privacy is not absolute in public schools, particularly in matters relating to school safety. Faced with violent crimes and substance abuse in hallways and classrooms, public schools are resorting to metal detectors, random locker searches, drug-sniffing dogs, and "zero tolerance" policies on knives and guns to protect students and preserve the educational environment.

After a student was stabbed to death by an intruder at Bayonne High School in Bayonne, New Jersey, in 1997, school officials installed surveillance cameras and required students to wear identification badges. In 1994 the school

"No, you want the lunch line. This is the search and seizure line."

board in the District of Columbia approved a policy allowing student lockers and desks to be searched at any time. In both cases, the school boards were attempting to improve student safety in the school as a whole, even though the boy whose face is caught on camera each morning when he walks into school or the girl whose desk is searched for no apparent reason is giving up some measure of personal privacy. Yet schools cannot ignore the privacy rights spelled out in the Fourth Amendment of the Bill of Rights. This important amendment limits government's power to intrude on the privacy of citizens without compelling circumstances. To conduct searches and seizures, police generally must have "probable cause" to believe they will find evidence of a crime.

Safety versus privacy

On February 6, 1997, the vice principal of Galt High School in Galt, California, entered a high school criminal justice class and asked the students to leave the classroom so drug-sniffing dogs could search their coats and backpacks. Senior Jacob Reed refused to give up his belongings and was taken to the principal's office, where he was searched. The dogs found no illegal items.

At the request of Reed, another student, and the classroom teacher, the American Civil Liberties Union filed suit against the school in U.S. district court in Sacramento, charging that random inspections by drug-sniffing dogs violate students' constitutional guarantees against unreasonable searches and seizures. "We would never tolerate that type of suspicionless search and seizure of adults. There's no reason why students should be forced to endure it," says attorney John Heller, representing the ACLU. Although Galt superintendent of schools Ron Huebert first defended the use of dogs to "provide a safe and drug-free environment," after much publicity the school board voted to end the program.

In this instance, the conflict was resolved before it went to court. But in other cases, courts have found that school officials, acting as both surrogate parents and educators,

A high school security guard uses a metal detector to search a student for weapons. Searches are allowed in schools because school safety is viewed as a higher priority than the right to privacy.

can sometimes put school safety above a student's right to privacy. School lockers and desks, and even cars parked in the school lot, are generally deemed school property, subject to random searches as long as students are informed of the policy. "The educator has the authority to implement the educational mission of the state and to do what it takes to make sure anything incompatible with the educational mission is discouraged," notes Bernard James, a professor of constitutional law at Pepperdine University and an authority on school safety.

Schools have generally based their search policies on a 1985 landmark Supreme Court decision in the case of *New Jersey v. T.L.O.*, a dispute over the search of a student's pocketbook. The Court ruled that students do have Fourth Amendment rights but that school searches are constitutional as long as "there is reasonable grounds for suspecting that the search will turn up evidence that the student has violated or is violating either the law or the rules of the school." This principle, known as "individualized suspicion," prevents random searches without cause.

Drug tests in the schools

The Court opened the door to student searches a little wider in 1995. The event that prompted this action involved James Acton, a seventh-grade Oregon boy who was banned from the football team because he would not take the urinalysis drug test required to participate in school sports. In *Vernonia School District 47J v. Acton*, the Court ruled the state's interest in attacking the problem of drugs in schools outweighs the student's right to "individualized suspicion." Thus, the Court approved random suspicionless drug testing for middle or high school athletes, even if school officials had no reason to suspect the individual athlete was using drugs.

The effect of this ruling on school safety programs remains to be seen. Several hundred schools now randomly test athletes and other students for substance abuse, reported the *New York Times* in 1997. Students at Piedmont High School in Piedmont, California, had to undergo a Breathalyzer analysis before attending the winter formal dance. "It was very controversial the first time around because it did seem like an intrusion. But I don't think the kids think it's that big a deal anymore," one parent told a *Times* reporter.

Ronald Stephens, director of the National School Safety Center, a private consulting group, recommends strict guidelines for school safety programs to ensure they are reasonable and treat all students equally. For example, California requires school metal detector programs to fairly apply standard search procedures to all students. The search must not be too intrusive for the age or sex of the child. "There needs to be some form of check or balance," Stephens says.

To educate and protect

When District of Columbia schools began allowing student lockers and desks to be searched at random in 1994, Tommy Brewer, the student representative to the D.C. Board of Education, responded that he did not want his school to become a prison. "I'm all for increased security.

But I want a private place to put my things. I don't have anything to hide. We can't treat students like criminals," Brewer stated in the *Washington Post*.

As this student observed, a school's task to educate and protect students without infringing on students' constitutional rights is a constant challenge. "In our system, state-operated schools may not be enclaves of totalitarianism. School officials do not possess absolute authority over their students. Students in school as well as out of school are 'persons' under our Constitution," wrote Supreme Court Justice Abe Fortas in the *Tinker* case in 1969. In the decades since Justice Fortas wrote these historic words, administrators and students have discovered just how difficult this balancing act can be.

3

Health Care: Who Decides?

CONFIDENTIALITY BETWEEN physician and patient is a basic tenet of the modern American health care system. A patient's medical records and conversations with a doctor should not be shared with anyone or made public without his or her permission. While some critics say the medical privacy laws, which vary from state to state, are inadequate in this era of computerized patient records, medical information and decisions about health care generally remain private matters between doctor and patient.

Yet persons under the age of eighteen are considered to lack the experience and judgment to make informed decisions about their health care. As a result, minors do not have the same right to privacy as adults. States, which regulate patient consent and confidentiality issues, typically hold parents legally responsible for their children's medical care. For example, a mother who fails to immunize her toddler may risk violating the state's child abuse laws. States also require the consent of a parent or other legal guardian before treating a minor, except in emergency situations when the child's life is at risk.

Yet a parent's right to decide a child's medical care must sometimes be balanced with other factors, such as a teenager's right to privacy or a child's health and safety.

Confidentiality for teenagers who choose to terminate a pregnancy is an intensely debated issue. Many states require that teens notify a parent or a judge before having an abortion. This requirement has led to tragedy on some occasions. In 1989, for example, an Indiana teenager named Becky Bell died of a septic infection from a botched illegal abortion. She did not want to disappoint her parents with news of her pregnancy, as required by state law, and so sought help from someone who did not require her parents' consent.

A minor's right to choose abortion

Few issues in American health care and public policy are as controversial as abortion. Some people feel abortion is a deeply personal decision that should not be legislated; others believe abortion is immoral and should be illegal. Prior to the early 1970s, state laws on abortion varied widely. Just four states, Alaska, Washington, New York, and Hawaii, permitted abortion for any reason until the point of fetal viability. Over 40 states permitted abortion only under certain circumstances, such as when the woman's life was in danger, while three states, Louisiana, New Hampshire, and Pennsylvania, prohibited abortion for any reason. Violaters of state abortion laws were criminally prosecuted in many states. Then in 1973, the Supreme Court decided in the landmark case *Roe v. Wade* that the Fourteenth Amendment's guarantee of personal liberty included the right to privacy for women who were deciding whether to continue a pregnancy. Thus, states could no longer interfere with a woman's decision to terminate a pregnancy within certain time limits.

But a teenager's constitutional right to terminate a pregnancy is qualified in many states by laws requiring that she first tell her parents. Since *Roe v. Wade*, states from Massachusetts to Indiana have passed laws mandating that minors notify a parent, secure a parent's written consent, or appear before a judge before having an abortion.

While teen abortion rates have declined since 1980, nearly 4 in 10 teen pregnancies end in abortion. There were about 308,000 abortions among teens in 1992, according to the Alan Guttmacher Institute, a nonprofit reproductive health research group. The majority of minors who have an abortion voluntarily tell at least one parent or responsible adult relative, teacher, or member of the clergy, according to the American Academy of Pediatrics.

Although parental consent laws find favor among a variety of people, opponents to legal abortion generally favor consent laws as part of a larger effort to limit abortions. Studies in Mississippi, Minnesota, and other states have shown that the number of minors having abortions drops after parental consent laws take effect. But the studies also

Antiabortion demonstrators protest on the third anniversary of the Supreme Court's Roe v. Wade *decision. Opinions on abortion, including a minor's right to privacy when seeking an abortion, remain divided.*

found that more minors sought abortions in neighboring states without consent laws.

Those who favor the laws also say teenagers lack the maturity to make informed decisions about abortion. A spokesman for the National Right to Life Committee told the *New York Times*, "Parents are the ones best able to guide their young children when faced with traumatic decisions."

Critics of parental consent laws, including the American Academy of Pediatrics and American Medical Association, say the laws cause pregnant teens to delay abortion, have a baby they do not want, go out of state, or undergo illegal abortion. "You cannot legislate how a family communicates. The desire of teenagers to maintain secrecy around sexual matters is so strong that they will often go to great lengths to protect those secrets," said Kate Michelman, the president of the National Abortion and Reproductive Rights Action League, in an interview with the *New York Times*.

While most people agree that teenagers can gain support and assistance by talking with their parents about this decision, some teenagers may worry about their parents' reaction, particularly in families with a history of violence. If the teen became pregnant through sexual abuse within the family, she has even more reason to fear causing a family crisis.

Nevertheless, the laws are favored by many states. As of 1997, twenty-eight states enforced parental notification or consent laws. But state laws vary widely, and even within states the laws are unevenly implemented by judges with more or less favorable views on abortion. "In Indianapolis, abortion clinics advise minors to go to Kentucky or Illinois, where such laws are not being enforced, rather than go before a [strict] judge in Indiana," writes Tamar Lewin in the *New York Times*.

Judicial bypass

Groups that support a woman's right to choose abortion have challenged consent laws in many states, and the Supreme Court has decided several cases with respect to a minor's right to abortion. In 1976 the justices held in *Planned Parenthood of Missouri v. Danforth* that parents do not have the power to arbitrarily veto the abortion decision of their minor daughters. In *Hodgson v. Minnesota* (1990), the justices upheld a Minnesota law requiring that both parents of a minor seeking an abortion be notified at least forty-eight hours before the abortion, but required the option of a "judicial bypass," a legal proceeding in which a teen can obtain authorization from a judge, instead.

A judicial bypass allows pregnant teens to petition a judge for an abortion without notifying a parent; the judge determines whether the teenager is mature enough to make the decision herself or if the abortion is in her best interest. Because of *Hodgson* and other similar high court decisions, many states with notification laws now include the option of a judicial bypass.

This issue remains divisive. In August 1997 a California court struck down a law passed ten years earlier requiring teenage girls to get the approval of a parent or judge before having an abortion. The court decided the law violated the right to privacy guaranteed to minors under California's state constitution.

Medical confidentiality for teens

In its guidelines for physicians who treat adolescents, the American Medical Association underscores the importance of doctor-patient confidentiality, not just for abortion services, but for all health care. Lack of confidentiality, or the perception of it, has been identified as a significant access barrier for adolescent health care. Some teens will not seek medical services, or talk openly with their physician about sensitive topics such as drug abuse or suicide, if their parents will be informed.

In fact, just as the Supreme Court and states began recognizing children's constitutional rights in education in the 1960s, they also began spelling out adolescents' rights in the health care system. For example, in 1977 the Supreme Court decided in *Carey v. Population Services International* that minors have the right to privacy when seeking contraceptives.

The windows of this Planned Parenthood clinic are bricked up in order to protect the safety and privacy of its patients. A minor's right to privacy when seeking reproductive health care is a controversial issue.

To tackle public health problems like unplanned teenage pregnancies and adolescent drug abuse, Congress and the states passed laws allowing minors to give informed consent to medical care without parental involvement, particularly for reproductive health, substance abuse, and mental health care. Informed consent means that the patient understands the risks and benefits of treatment and any alternatives that may exist, and is able to make a choice among the alternatives.

As a result of these laws, states now generally allow minors to make their own decisions when seeking diagnosis and treatment of sexually transmitted diseases. By 1995 almost all states had laws authorizing a minor with a drug or alcohol problem to obtain confidential medical care and counseling. In addition, certain groups of minors are generally allowed to give consent for their own medical treatment. Depending on the state, these may include teenagers

living apart from their families, married teenagers, teenagers who are parents, and high school graduates. Some states also have laws giving "mature minors," or older adolescents, significant legal rights in medical decisions. Even without "mature minor" laws, states usually allow doctors to treat adolescents over the age of fifteen who are capable of giving informed consent, especially if treatment poses little risk.

However, adolescent confidentiality is not absolute, according to a 1994 report by the National Center for Youth Law. Many states have minimum age limits, varying from twelve to fifteen, under which parents must be involved in most medical decisions. Sometimes, state laws and regulations, court decisions, and professional ethical standards differ on what information is confidential or what conditions qualify as exceptions and can be reported.

Some states also give doctors the option of informing parents in general terms that their son or daughter has sought medical attention. Also, in certain situations doctors actually may be required to disclose information, such as in the case of suspected physical or sexual abuse, or if the teenager poses a severe danger to himself or others.

AIDS testing and treatment

The AIDS epidemic prompts new questions about an adolescent's right to confidential medical care. Through June 1995, a total of 2,184 AIDS cases among thirteen- to nineteen-year-olds was reported to the federal Centers for Disease Control and Prevention. Yet adolescents may be reluctant to be tested and treated for HIV infection if they believe their parents or others will be notified. Teens who use drugs or are sexually active, known risk factors for the virus, may fear their parents' disapproval of their behavior.

Adults are assured confidentiality at HIV test sites and in deciding treatment with their doctors, but a minor's rights to confidential AIDS testing and treatment vary from state to state. Some thirty-two states allow minors to make their own decisions about testing and treatment without parental consent, according to a 1995 report by the AIDS

Policy Center at George Washington University. However, some states do not require confidentiality of test results for minors. For example, Colorado allows minors to consent to testing, but permits physicians to disclose the HIV test or treatment information to parents or legal guardians if the minor is under sixteen.

Since the mid-1990s, successful new drug therapies for AIDS have brought fresh hope to people with AIDS. One outgrowth of the scientific advances has been a push for less secrecy surrounding the disease. In the near future, the confidentiality rights of people of all ages in HIV testing and treatment may be outweighed by the medical benefits of detecting the disease early and tracking its course. Some health experts and AIDS advocates now believe the names of HIV positive persons should be reported to public health departments so that states can follow the disease better and offer treatment to those who need it. In the future, mandatory reporting of the disease could also require people with HIV or AIDS to inform public health officials of their sexual partners or drug sharers so that those people also have access to early testing and treatment. In 1997, a bill was introduced in Congress that would require states to report all HIV cases to the federal government and also inform anyone who has been exposed to the virus.

Advocates for AIDS patients are generally opposed to forcing patients of any age to disclose their illness, because people may avoid getting tested or become vulnerable to discrimination. But, they say, the recent advances in AIDS treatment may change attitudes toward confidentiality and privacy for people with the disease. "Everything is changing so rapidly right now that most of us are in a position of having to re-evaluate everything we held gospel for many years," said Cleve Jones, a prominent gay activist.

Reproductive health services in school

Schools in the 1990s are an important resource for information about the AIDS virus. But medical confidentiality becomes more complicated in public schools. When a teenager seeks health services on campus, his or her right to privacy is balanced by the school's obligations to both inform parents about their child's health and meet community standards regarding sensitive issues like teenage sexual activity.

There is little doubt that students need all the information they can get. Every year, 3 million teenagers acquire a sexually transmitted disease, including HIV, and 1 million teenage girls become pregnant, most of them unintentionally. Responding to this serious public health crisis, some schools offer reproductive health counseling and services at school-based clinics.

School health services, unlike health care in a doctor's office or clinic, are often restricted in the information and services they can provide. Also, state confidentiality laws may not apply in schools, which set their own policies, often according to parental and community opinion.

After a mother complained that a county social worker gave her teenage son and his girlfriend advice about abortion on the grounds of Potomac High School in 1996, the Prince William County School Board in Virginia enacted a regulation prohibiting school staff from discussing abortion with students. Instead, inquiries are to be referred to

High school students pass a petition to allow condom distribution in schools. School health clinics are often barred from offering information and services, including contraception.

an agency off the school grounds. The school district also requires staff to inform parents or a social services agency if a student discloses she is pregnant.

School-based reproductive health services, as well as sex education, remain controversial. Many people fear that schools may be endorsing or encouraging teens to engage in sex without enough emphasis on abstinence. Yet school officials want to provide potentially lifesaving assistance to students engaging in risky behavior. Policies that restrict information or health services may prevent students from getting the help they need. "If we set up too many barriers, the kids won't bring problems to anyone, and the problems will fester," said Anne Terrell, who oversees the Prince William County school nurses, in the *Washington Post*.

Condom distribution

Thirteen states prohibit or restrict school-based health programs from providing abortion counseling or referrals,

according to a 1995 report by the National Abortion Rights and Action League. Similarly, in 1995, North Carolina joined some nineteen states in banning the distribution of contraceptives on school property.

The debate over school condom distribution programs raises similar questions about a student's access to reproductive health services in schools. Voluntary condom distribution programs, developed in hundreds of schools in the past decade to stop the spread of AIDS and prevent pregnancies, have been challenged by parents concerned that they condone or encourage teen sex and violate the parents' right to guide their children. In some cities, parents went to court to keep their children from participating.

In 1995, Massachusetts was the first state to decide that providing condoms to students on a voluntary basis does not interfere with parents' religious freedom nor with their right to raise their children as they see fit, reported John Ellement in the *Boston Globe*. In 1991, the town of Falmouth, Massachusetts, with help from the Massachusetts Department of Public Health, made condoms available in the schools as a way of battling AIDS and other sexually transmitted diseases. Students are able to buy condoms from vending machines or request them from school health staff. The program is combined with sex education stressing abstinence, according to a lawyer for the Falmouth School Committee, which supports the program.

A violation of parental rights?

But four families from Falmouth filed suit against the schools, claiming that the program violates their First Amendment right to religious expression, sends the message that premarital sex is okay, and interferes with the privacy rights of the family. "The condom policy . . . is today the singly most offensive in the country in its total ban on parental input into the decision to provide these devices to their children," Larry L. Crain, the attorney for the families, wrote in a court brief. Over forty other communities in the state also rejected condoms as part of a comprehensive AIDS curriculum.

Two seventeen-year-olds display a condom they obtained through a distribution program at their high school.

The American Civil Liberties Union, representing the schools, argued that the students had a right to the condoms and related information. "We feel it's very important that minors' privacy rights be protected and that with the grave crisis of teen pregnancy and the AIDS epidemic, schools be permitted to respond to those crises in appropriate ways," said the ACLU's Jennifer Brown.

In his decision in *Elizabeth G. Curtis v. School of Falmouth*, Chief Justice Paul J. Liacos of the Supreme Judicial Court stated that the program is voluntary and does not take away parents' right to advise their children about religious and moral issues. "Mere exposure to programs offered at school does not amount to an unconstitutional interference with parental liberties," he declared. The Supreme Court refused to review the case in 1996, and the program continues.

When religion clashes with medicine

Most parents believe that they are best suited for deciding important issues that involve their child's health. Yet a parent's religious or personal beliefs can sometimes even cause a child harm. When sixteen-year-old Shannon Nixon, of Altoona, Pennsylvania, began feeling weak and thirsty in June 1995, her parents took her to her grandfather, a pastor in the Faith Tabernacle congregation, a Christian sect founded in 1897 in Philadelphia. The congregation believes that disease comes from the devil and that God, not medicine, cures illness. Although no one knew what was wrong with Shannon, the family did not call a doctor. They relied, instead, on the prayers of the congregation.

In less than a week, Shannon fell into a diabetic coma and died of a heart attack caused by untreated diabetes. In 1997, her parents were found guilty of involuntary manslaughter and endangering the welfare of a child.

Despite the public indignation that follows extreme incidents such as this, forty-six states have religious exemption laws that protect parents who use spiritual treatment to cure their child's illness in accordance with the beliefs of a recognized religion, such as Christian Science. The laws shield parents from prosecution for child abuse and neglect in these cases, but some states also mandate that parents' religious rights should not limit a child's medical care in life-threatening situations.

In 1993 the Massachusetts Supreme Judicial Court overturned the manslaughter conviction of a Christian Science couple in the death of their two-year-old son. Christian Scientists believe in spiritual healing, rather than medicine, to treat illness. Thus, the couple relied on a Christian Science healer, not a doctor, when the boy fell ill with a bowel obstruction. The boy died and the couple was convicted of manslaughter. But the couple appealed the decision, and the higher court cited the state's religious exemption statute as relieving the couple from guilt. Soon after, Massachusetts joined Hawaii, Maryland, and South Dakota in repealing the law protecting parents in these cases.

Access to health care

The American Academy of Pediatrics declared in 1997 that the Constitution's guarantee of religious freedom does not permit children to be harmed or allow religion to be a defense when a parent harms or neglects a child. "This is not a religious issue at all. It's a fundamental matter of children's rights," said Dr. Joel Fader, chairman of the Academy's Bioethics Committee, in an interview. "There should be equal access of all children to medical treatment and that shouldn't vary based on the religious views of the parents."

In general, children benefit from the advice and support of their parents in matters involving their health. Yet not all families are able to discuss openly such sensitive issues as abortion or AIDS, and many states have recognized that sometimes a minor's need for medical services outweighs a parent's right to be informed. By knowing their legal rights to confidential medical care in their state, teenagers will be better prepared to seek the health care they need.

4

Children and
Their Families

ON MONDAY, MARCH 31, 1997, New Yorkers awoke to tragic headlines in their morning newspapers. Five-year-old Daytwon Bennett had died of child abuse syndrome, neglect, and starvation. His mother had delivered her son's lifeless body to a Bronx hospital. Daytwon lived with his mother and five brothers and sisters in a spotless apartment in the Bronx, according to reports. The city caseworker who visited the home just nine days before had not found the boy was in danger.

Daytwon was the latest in a horrifying series of children chronically neglected and fatally injured by their parents in New York City. Seven months earlier, four-year-old Nadine Lockwood was starved to death by her mother, a drug abuser who lived in extreme poverty with seven children. In November 1995, Elisa Izquierdo, age six, was beaten to death by her drug-addicted mother. "Something like this shouldn't happen. We're all accountable," New York mayor Rudolph Giuliani told *Newsweek* after Elisa's death.

Behind the headlines

Despite laws that protect children from unfit parents, sometimes child abuse goes undetected until it is too late. In 1995, approximately 1,215 children were killed as a result of abuse or neglect, usually at the hands of people whom they loved and trusted, according to the National Committee to Prevent Child Abuse, a nonprofit advocacy organization.

Not making newspaper headlines, but still shocking, were the more than 500,000 children chronically neglected by their parents that year, according to federal figures.

Many child advocates believe the problem is not the lack of legal protections for children at risk, but the failure of the child welfare system to do its job. In some states, the social service system designed to protect children from maltreatment is overburdened and understaffed, letting even children known to be vulnerable to fall through the cracks. "You can't avoid every tragedy, but you can do better than we are doing," acknowledged Nicholas Scoppetta, the commissioner of the Administration for Children's Services in New York City, to a *New York Times* reporter.

Yet child protection laws and the child welfare system do save lives. A few months before Daytwon's death, a

The small coffin of Nadine Lockwood, a four-year-old starved to death by her mother in 1996, is wheeled past media and mourners in New York.

Brooklyn woman and her boyfriend were arrested after they left four of her children unattended for six hours, according to news reports. Someone called 911 and told police that the children were left home alone. The police responded immediately. The mother and boyfriend were charged with endangering the welfare of her children; and the children, who were not harmed, were placed in foster care.

Protecting those who cannot protect themselves

A child's right to be cared for is fundamental in this country. Children rely first on their parents for such basics as shelter, food, health care, and education. When parents cannot meet these basic needs, society steps in through laws and social services. Since the 1960s, state and federal laws have been put in place to safeguard children in families and guarantee their rights when they are removed from families because of inadequate care.

In 1962, C. Henry Kempe and his colleagues at the University of Colorado School of Medicine published an article titled "The Battered-Child Syndrome" in the *Journal of the American Medical Association*. Kempe had been studying abuse and neglect in young children for over a decade and had discovered that not only was child abuse a larger problem than most people knew, but also that nobody was really responsible for reporting or preventing it.

Kempe urged physicians to report child maltreatment and asked the government to formulate a better system to protect children. During the 1970s, the federal government and the states established child abuse treatment and prevention programs and passed child abuse reporting laws.

Reporting laws

Today all fifty states have laws requiring professionals who work with children to report suspected child abuse or neglect to police or local child protective agencies. The National Center on Child Abuse and Neglect at the U.S. Department of Health and Human Services defines child abuse as the physical or mental injury, sexual abuse, negligent treatment, or maltreatment of a child under eighteen by a person responsible for the child's welfare under circumstances that indicate that the child's health or welfare is harmed or threatened.

Teachers, school nurses, and day-care workers are trained to look out for the child who comes to school with unexplained bruises, burns, or other injuries, or who seems hungry or inadequately dressed, or who has serious behavior problems possibly related to maltreatment. When they suspect a child is being abused or neglected, they must notify the police or the local child protective services agency. In fact, any citizen with "reasonable suspicion" should contact authorities and file a report, and they can do so anonymously. All states have laws shielding the reporter of suspected abuse or neglect from legal liability, unless the call was made maliciously.

The number of children reported for abuse or neglect has risen sharply in the past twenty years, from 669,000 in 1976 to 2,900,000 in 1994, according to the National Center

A school official points to the poor attendance record of a student who has suffered neglect. School staff members are trained to respond to such indications of abuse or neglect.

on Child Abuse and Neglect. During the 1980s, the crack cocaine epidemic and the havoc the drug created in families contributed to an increase in child maltreatment.

Some people have criticized reporting laws for allowing people to file false reports, which may unfairly stigmatize parents who are not mistreating their children. Not surprisingly, not every report of suspected abuse is substantiated. About one-third, or 1,012,000 children, of the

The stories of maltreated children evoke an emotional response from the public. Here, a demonstrator urges people to take a stand against abuse.

2.9 million reported were found to be the victims of abuse or neglect in 1994.

Also, reporting laws are successful only when adults who suspect child abuse follow through with their legal duty to notify authorities. A seven-year-old girl arrived at her Brooklyn, New York, elementary school at least six times with black-and-blue marks on her face, an open wound on her head, and a burn mark on her hand. While many school employees had noticed the girl's condition and even discussed it, it took nine months for the school to report the case to the state's child abuse hotline in May 1997, according to news reports. "While it is hard to imagine a mother inflicting such pain on her child, the inaction and indifference of school authorities is equally incomprehensible," said one school official to the *New York Times*. The mother was later arrested and the girl was placed in foster care.

Determining child abuse or neglect

Once the authorities receive a call alleging that a child is being maltreated, they will ask the person making the report questions to determine whether or not abuse or neglect has occurred. If the suspicions appear legitimate, they will send an investigating team, and perhaps the police, to assess the family situation.

Every community has a child protective services agency with the legal authority to evaluate allegations of child abuse and neglect. The agency examines the home and interviews the parents, child, and other witnesses to determine if sufficient cause exists to warrant some action and intervention by the agency.

The child welfare system is primarily interested in preventing further harm of the child and helping parents overcome their problems so that they can provide a safe and loving home. If the investigators find a child is not in imminent danger, they may decide he or she should remain in the home, with regular visits from a caseworker to make sure the situation is improving. In most cases, troubled families are given assistance such as counseling, parent training, financial support, or other social services.

If child welfare workers believe a child's health and safety cannot be guaranteed at home, they will remove the child and place him or her with a relative or in foster care pending further investigation. This happens in about 15 percent of the cases of proven maltreatment. Thus, the child is temporarily in a safe environment while the authorities look for a permanent solution.

When Chicago police found nineteen hungry and unhealthy children in a cold apartment in February 1994, child protection workers quickly took the children from the six women who were their mothers and put them in foster homes while the Cook County juvenile court began proceedings to investigate the mothers' behavior and decide the children's futures.

In extreme cases of abuse, such as the death of Daytwon Bennett, the police arrest the parent, since a parent who critically harms a son or daughter is just as liable for criminal prosecution as a stranger. Criminal abuse and neglect has a higher burden of proof than civil abuse and neglect, and criminal abuse charges are processed through the criminal court system.

Family court

In noncriminal but serious cases of abuse and neglect, the child protective agency files a petition in family court to protect the minor by taking custody or imposing certain requirements on the parents. Family court is a noncriminal court with jurisdiction over family issues, including divorce, domestic violence, juvenile delinquency, and child custody issues. The court's aim is to protect the child from harm and help parents overcome their problems and provide a good home.

In some states, family court proceedings are closed to the public to protect the privacy of the children and parents, but this tradition may be changing. In 1997, Chief Judge Judith Kaye set new rules for New York State's Family Court, opening it up to the public for the first time to help make the child protective system less hidden and more accountable.

Federal law requires children in abuse and neglect court proceedings to have a legal representative, either a lawyer or a guardian ad litem, a lawyer or volunteer charged with representing the child's best interests. "This is the sole person in court who is totally, exclusively representing the child," says Mark Hardin, an attorney with the American Bar Association's Center on Children and the Law. Child advocates stress the importance of the child's having a voice in court, since both the parent and the protective services agency are represented by attorneys. Without an adult advocate of the child's interests, the court might not grasp his or her viewpoint or needs, which may contradict the parent's. But despite federal requirements, not every child is represented in court in every state, says Hardin. State budget constraints and a lack of recognition that children need their own advocate have contributed to this problem. There are only enough people to do this job for 25 percent of children who need them, according to the national Court Appointed Special Advocate Association in Seattle.

The American Bar Association is concerned about the poor representation of children in family court. "In child abuse and neglect cases, the legal representation of parents, children, and child protection agencies is often seriously deficient. It is not unusual for attorneys for parties to be absent from hearings that can determine parental rights to visitation, custody, and services concerning their children," stated ABA president N. Lee Cooper at the ABA's meeting in San Antonio, Texas, in February 1997.

Foster care

After hearing testimony from all sides, the family court judge makes a decision based on the child's best interest. If the judge determines the parents cannot care for their child, the state assumes temporary legal custody and the child is placed in foster care. There are many reasons why a child may be in foster care besides abuse and neglect. A parent may be too ill or financially destitute to keep the child at home, or a parent may be unable to control a troubled adolescent.

In 1996, 502,000 children were living in substitute care, up from 262,000 in 1982, according to the American Public Welfare Association. These children may be in a group home or institution or in an individual foster family home. Foster homes are licensed by the state and supervised by the child protective agency; foster parents undergo background checks and provide character references before being licensed to take in foster children. They receive a monthly stipend to cover the costs of caring for the child.

Children in foster care have certain legal rights that must be protected. The state must make certain the child receives adequate food, clothing, housing, education, and medical treatment. The child also has the right not to be abused or neglected in the foster care system. The child's court-appointed lawyer or advocate is responsible for acting on behalf of the child if these rights are threatened.

Although most children in foster care are well treated, sometimes the system fails, as when a four-year-old New York City girl died, malnourished, beaten, and bruised, in a foster home in 1997. The private foster care agency that

hired the foster mother was warned by another agency that she might not be a good parent because children in her care in the past were not properly cared for. But no such report was on file at the state office that catalogs abuse and neglect complaints. "This was a tragedy, that with further investigation, could have been avoided," said Todd Silverblatt, senior attorney at Legal Aid's Juvenile Rights Division, which represented the child in family court, in the *New York Times*.

No one—not the foster family's caseworker nor the Legal Aid attorney who represented the child—had noticed anything was wrong in the home, according to the *Times*.

Deciding the future

Federal foster care policy requires that states have a plan, with goals for the future, for every child in substitute care. The state must regularly review the child's case, either to reunite the family as soon as possible or make sure the foster care placement is working. If the placement is not appropriate, then the child has the right to move to a better situation. For example, the child should be living close enough to his or her biological parents to be able to see them regularly, if possible.

For nearly 70 percent of foster children, foster care is temporary and they eventually return to their natural family, according to the American Public Welfare Association. But when a parent is unable to resolve his or her problems, such as drug addiction or mental illness, the child may languish in foster care for months, years, or even until adulthood. Long-term foster care is considered detrimental because of the insecurity and uncertainty it causes the child.

Seeking to put a time limit on foster care, child welfare policy has seesawed between two philosophies: family reunification—that is, returning the child to the biological parent—and permanent placement for children in adoptive families. In the 1980s, child welfare policy favored keeping families together when possible, both to reduce the strain on the foster care system and to counter the perception that child welfare agencies were removing children from their parents without sufficient proof of maltreatment.

This poster is part of a campaign to urge people to report child abuse before it escalates to death.

Yet this policy ignored the need to protect children at risk, some critics believe, and sometimes children returned too soon to troubled homes were subjected to more abuse. "A number of people feel that this philosophy has put children back into dangerous situations," says Charles Phipps, an attorney with the national Center for Prosecution of Child Abuse. Daytwon Bennett and his siblings were repeatedly removed from their mother's care because of maltreatment, but they were returned home after she had counseling. Daytwon eventually lost his life.

Unfortunately, not all families can be put back together, even with counseling and support from social services professionals. Sometimes, parents and children are better off apart. "All families can't be saved," comments Marcia

Robinson Lowry, head of the Children's Rights Project, a legal advocacy group in New York. In these cases, Lowry and others advocate taking swift action to find a permanent, safe home for the child.

Terminating parental rights

Because of cases like Daytwon's and the belief that every child has a right to a permanent home, the 1990s saw new efforts to make adoption easier for the minority of foster children whose biological parents will probably never be able to care for them. In recent years, only about 8 percent of children who leave foster care are adopted, the American Public Welfare Association reports. Also, it takes an average of one to six years for children to be legally free for adoption, and that is too long, according to many advocates.

In 1997, Congress was considering an important bill to allow states to move children out of foster care more quickly and increase adoptions. While current law requires states to make "reasonable efforts" to help and preserve the biological family before considering adoption, this would no longer be required in the worst cases of abandonment or repeated abuse. Most of these children have been in foster care much of their lives, some even from birth, and permanent placement with a relative or adoption is the best alternative.

For a child to be free for adoption, the biological parent's legal rights to the child must be terminated. This happens only after a parent has repeatedly or seriously maltreated a child or cannot care for the child for another reason such as mental illness. The family court judge must find the parent unfit and decide that termination is in the child's best interest. This ends the parent's legal relationship to the child.

By the time a parent's rights are terminated, the family is usually already fractured. Often, parents and children no longer have a relationship. *Chicago Tribune* reporter Louise Kiernan described the case of a mother who lost custody of her children in 1992. She had rarely seen them since. When the thirty-minute hearing to permanently end

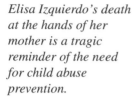

Elisa Izquierdo's death at the hands of her mother is a tragic reminder of the need for child abuse prevention.

her parental rights took place in 1997, neither she, the children's fathers, nor the children were present, just their lawyers and the children's caseworker.

Inadequate protection

Child maltreatment will not go away on its own. To guarantee every child a safe home, child abuse reports have to be investigated and child protection laws must be enforced, say child advocates. The agencies that monitor and help troubled families need the staff and resources to do their job and spot dangerous situations before tragedy occurs. "Fixing the system won't be cheap. But is child protection really where we want to look for budget cuts, as we've done in the past?" write child abuse policy experts David Stoesz and Howard Jacob Karger in the *Washington Monthly*.

After Elisa Izquierdo died in 1995, New York City overhauled the city's child welfare agency. Six hundred new caseworkers were hired and trained and a new computer system was put in place. Yet in 1997, the agency was still not adequately protecting children, a court-appointed review panel found. In almost a third of the child abuse reports, the agency failed to determine whether a child was safe within twenty-four hours of the reported abuse, as required by law.

5

Children at Work

BEHIND THE DELI counter at the local supermarket, a sixteen-year-old boy pushes turkey through the meat slicing machine, while a twenty-year-old woman pours flour into the power dough mixer. This everyday work scene may look harmless to customers, but one of these employees is working illegally at a dangerous job.

Adults and teenagers may share the same workplace and hold similar jobs in the United States, but the labor laws protecting the two groups and giving them certain rights are very different. While the twenty-year-old is permitted to operate the power dough mixer, her young coworker cannot legally run the meat slicer, which is considered too dangerous for workers under eighteen. Likewise, if their boss asked them to work after 7 P.M. on a school night, only the older worker could legally do so.

Over 6 million teenagers took home paychecks in 1996, according to the U.S. Department of Labor. The majority of teenagers work for retailers, like fast-food franchises, while others are employed in agriculture, forestry, fisheries, manufacturing, and construction. For the most part, young workers are treated no differently than adults in the same jobs. They must hold Social Security cards, pay taxes on income above a certain amount, and follow their employer's rules.

Yet federal and state labor laws impose strict rules on child labor, defined as the employment of children under eighteen. In the United States, an estimated 2.4 million young people ages fifteen to seventeen work during the school year and 3.3 million during the summer. When child labor laws are not followed, these young workers are put in jeopardy.

The Fair Labor Standards Act

The Fair Labor Standards Act, or FLSA, gives the Department of Labor the authority to regulate child labor in the areas of minimum age, hours, and hazardous work. Congress passed the historic employment law in 1938 as part of the New Deal, President Franklin D. Roosevelt's effort to rebuild the economy and create jobs to end the Great Depression.

The law, which has changed little in more than half a century, helped to better the lives of all workers, especially children. For example, the minimum wage was set at twenty-five cents an hour and the work week was limited to forty hours. Prior to 1938, children were allowed to work long hours in factories, mills, mines, sweatshops, and other unsafe workplaces. The FLSA did not eliminate child labor, but rather established rules and standards to protect minors. Even more important, employers of young

A young girl works at a factory spinning machine. The Fair Labor Standards Act prevented children from doing this and other work considered unsafe.

workers knew the federal government could fine or even arrest them for violations.

Under the law, young people must be at least sixteen to hold most jobs in nonagricultural industries. Fourteen- and fifteen-year-olds may hold certain jobs in retail, food service, and other businesses, but only after school and no more than three hours in a school day and eighteen hours in a school week. When school is out, fourteen- and fifteen-year-olds can work up to eight hours a day and forty hours a week. They cannot work before 7 A.M. or after 7 P.M. during the school year and 9 P.M. in the summer. Children who are twelve and older, and even age ten in some states, can baby-sit, deliver newspapers, caddy at a golf course, or do nonhazardous work for their parents, but not during school hours.

Federal and state laws

The federal law, enforced by the Wage and Hour Division of the Employment Standards Administration in the Labor Department, includes the Hazardous Occupations Orders, which prohibit children under eighteen from working in coal mines, driving delivery vehicles, operating power saws, handling toxins, operating forklifts, and performing certain other dangerous jobs.

Also important is the federal Occupational Safety and Health Administration (OSHA), which sets workplace safety standards to protect workers from fire and electrical dangers, chemical hazards, machinery accidents, and other on-the-job risks. OSHA enforces its standards through inspections and follow-ups on worker complaints. Penalties can range from $7,000 for serious violations to $70,000 for willful violations of safety and health standards.

In addition, many states impose stricter child labor laws than the federal government. New York, with some of the strongest labor laws in the country, limits working hours for sixteen- and seventeen-year-olds during the school year, while the federal government does not. New York also orders educational authorities to revoke employment certificates or working papers when a student fails four academic courses in one semester, while the federal law has no such requirement. Employers must follow whichever standard is higher, the state or federal law.

In all states, minors who want to work are required to have employment certificates or permits through their school districts, and proof of age, written permission from parents, and health certificates are usually required.

Violations of child labor laws

While the child labor laws in the United States are among the most strict in the world, children are still at risk in the workplace. Young workers may not be aware of their rights, and employers can take advantage of their inexperience and ignore the laws. "Unlike some Third World countries, we don't have children chained to desks or worktables. But we do have our own problems in this country and they are serious ones," said Jeffrey Newman, executive director of the National Child Labor Committee, a private nonprofit organization founded in 1904 to end child labor. Employers, not young workers, are responsible for obeying child labor laws.

A significant number of children still work illegally in the United States. Under pressure from children's advocates, the Labor Department conducted sweeps in the early 1990s to uncover illegal child labor. In March 1990, the department led a nationwide raid on supermarkets, fast-food restaurants, garment industry operations, and other businesses suspected of child labor abuses. Operation Child Watch, as it was called, found seven thousand minors working illegally and violations in nearly half the businesses, reported *Newsweek*. Because of these sweeps, in fiscal year 1990 the Department of Labor found 39,790 minors illegally employed, compared to 9,968 in 1980.

As a major employer of adolescents, supermarkets have often run afoul of the labor laws. In 1993, the Labor Department found more than nine hundred child labor violations in 106 A&P grocery stores, and fined the company $490,000. In stores in five states, minors were found operating paper balers, meat cutters, and power dough mixers,

dangerous machines off-limits to young workers; fourteen-
and fifteen-year-olds were working at illegal hours and
longer than allowed by law; and twelve- and thirteen-year-
olds were employed illegally. At least four other national
supermarket chains paid fines in 1993 and 1994 for similar
violations.

The fast-food industry, which also relies on unskilled,
part-time and minimum-wage labor, is another major employer of teenagers. In 1990, Congress held a hearing on
fast-food restaurants, including McDonald's, Burger King,
Little Caesar's, and Domino's Pizza. These companies, or
their franchises, allowed children to work too long, without permits, or during school hours, or they hired underage
workers. Then in 1992, the Labor Department fined Burger
King $500,000 for letting fourteen- and fifteen-year-olds
work past 7 P.M. on school nights.

Since the early 1990s, many major fast-food companies
and supermarkets have stopped hiring underage workers
and made sure teenagers do not perform hazardous jobs or
work too late, according to the Labor Department and children's advocates. "We've been checking them and we're
seeing them in compliance," said Bill Fern, a labor analyst
at the Wage and Hour Division. By the mid-1990s, the

*Fast-food restaurants,
which commonly
employ teenagers, are
strictly regulated to
avoid child labor
violations.*

department recorded fewer child labor violations. In fiscal year 1996, investigators found 7,376 young workers in 1,714 businesses in violation of child labor laws, and assessed $6.8 million in penalties. Repeat violations can lead to criminal penalties.

The underground economy

Fast-food and grocery businesses have come under pressure to improve labor practices, but the underground economy, or businesses that evade paying taxes or following labor regulations, are notorious for illegal child labor. Door-to-door candy selling is one of those businesses, usually employing young urban children eager to make a few extra dollars, reports Brian Dumaine in *Fortune* magazine. "These candy companies break just about every child labor law on the books," said Mary Pedretti, a police officer in Vallejo, California. Vans pick up children as young as seven after school and drive them to neighborhoods, sometimes far from home, to sell candy to strangers for $5 a box. The children keep $1 for each box. "The driver would have 20 kids in his van," an eleven-year-old girl told *Fortune*. "We'd usually sit on the floor. There were no seat

A fifteen-year-old girl in New York works on clothing during school hours. The garment industry employs many children who work long hours for low pay.

belts. . . . One time we were in Livermore, 50 miles away, and I didn't get home until 3:30 in the morning."

Children also illegally work in the garment industry, often in underground apparel sweatshops, which often hire new immigrants who cannot find other jobs. In New York, Miami, San Francisco, Houston, and other major cities, underage children skip school to operate high-speed sewing machines, press fabrics, and cut threads in clothing sweatshops, according to the National Child Labor Committee. "It's a problem that's getting worse," said Newman.

A 1991 report in the *New Yorker* described children in Manhattan's Chinatown who work alongside their mothers in unventilated, lint-filled rooms. "The worst are basement shops. No exit doors," a member of the Department of Labor's Apparel Industry Task Force told the magazine. "Child labor working fifty to sixty hours a week for three dollars and twenty five cents an hour, under minimum wage. No records whatsoever. No overtime. No time cards. No ventilation. I've seen eight- and nine-year-olds working in these basements." The task force enforces state labor laws in seven thousand garment factories, including these small sweatshops.

Children on the farm

Far from the urban sweatshops, thousands of children pick fruit and vegetables, operate heavy machinery, and tend large animals on farms. Estimates of children in agriculture range from 250,000 to 800,000, yet farmwork has the most lenient child labor laws of all industries. Back in 1938, Congress bowed to pressures from farmers who relied on their families' labor, and exempted agriculture from most child labor laws.

Children as young as twelve can work outside school hours on commercial farms, if their parents are employed by the farm, and fourteen-year-olds can perform almost all agricultural work. While other workers must be eighteen to perform hazardous jobs, sixteen-year-old farmworkers can operate grain combines, work in stalls occupied by bulls or horses, unload timber, and apply pesticides.

A ten-year-old boy feeds a calf on a farm in North Carolina. Minors working on their families' farms are the least restricted of all child laborers.

Even the federal Hazardous Occupations Order does not apply to minors employed on a farm owned or operated by their parents. Children cannot get driver's licenses until their sixteenth birthday in most states, but they can drive a parent's tractor at age eleven or even younger. In fact, family farms have the fewest restrictions. Minors may work at any age, with parental consent, on their family's farm, despite the dangers of working with heavy machinery, livestock, and agricultural chemicals.

Migrant farmworkers

Perhaps the worst working conditions in the United States are endured by migrant farmworkers, who travel to find work picking fruits and vegetables. "The next time you buy fresh fruit or vegetables from the supermarket, think about the true costs. Rosa Rubina will," notes Ron Nixon in the *Progressive*. "Her five-year-old son Jacob lost his hand while helping to grade and package watermelons in Tifton, Georgia. The boy's hand was caught in a conveyor belt and ripped off." Rubina, a migrant worker, had tried to get her son into day care, but the waiting list was too long so she had him work with her.

Despite efforts by farmworkers unions, children of migrant workers continue to be exposed to agricultural pesticides, substandard housing, inadequate health care, and poor sanitation. "Migrant and seasonal farmworkers are not given the same protection as other minors," says Darlene Adkins, coordinator of the Child Labor Coalition, an advocacy group. Very young children illegally help their parents in the fields, since every extra bushel means more food on the table. "On any given day during the harvest season, children as young as five are in the field picking cucumbers, tomatoes, strawberries, and other hand-harvested fruits," observes Nixon. Nearly half of migrant children quit school before graduating from high school.

Politicians from farm states are under pressure not to change the labor laws, since farmers may rely on their children or migrant labor to keep costs down. But advocates for migrant workers want more protection for the children. "Although children have been a good source of cheap

Young children work alongside their parents picking produce in a field. Like their parents, the children of migrant farmworkers often work in dangerous and unsanitary conditions.

labor, over time our society has committed itself to protecting children from neglect, abuse, and exploitation. . . . And just how is this different for the migrant farmworker child than for other children?" asks Diane Mull, executive director of the Association of Farmworker Opportunity Programs, which provides employment, training, and other services to farmworkers.

Injuries on the job

Back strains, wrist strains, and lacerations are common injuries to children on farms, and preteens are more likely to be severely injured in agriculture than in other industries. Yet even in nonagricultural jobs, young workers, often inexperienced and less knowledgeable about equipment, are injured at a higher rate than adults.

In 1992, sixty-four thousand adolescents required treatment in hospital emergency rooms for work-related injuries, and sixty-eight workers under eighteen died, primarily in agricultural and retail industries, according to the National Institute for Occupational Safety and Health (NIOSH). Of job-related adolescent deaths between 1980 and 1989, motor vehicle–related accidents accounted for nearly one quarter, followed by operating tractors and other heavy equipment, electrical hazards, and assaults and violent attacks, usually associated with robberies, reported NIOSH. More than 50 percent of teen occupational injuries occur in the retail industry, according to the Department of Labor.

The American Academy of Pediatrics has found that employment during childhood and adolescence carries risks for serious injuries such as amputations, burns, scalds, scalpings, fractures, eye loss, and electrocution. "Although there are positive benefits to youth employment, it's important to realize that work can be a hazardous environment," said Dawn Castillo, an epidemiologist at NIOSH.

Preventing tragedy

When labor laws are ignored, workers are more likely to be injured. According to the *Los Angeles Times*, in a recent study of young workers NIOSH found that 70 percent of deaths involved violations of federal child labor laws. In 1988, a fifteen-year-old boy in Clifton, Virginia, was working for a general contractor, spreading tar over newly installed insulation on a roof. He stepped on the tar paper covering a skylight opening in the roof, and fell to his death twenty-five feet below. The Labor Department found the boy was illegally performing a hazardous job.

NIOSH recommends employers be familiar with labor laws and occupational safety and health regulations, and not ask young workers to do dangerous tasks. To prevent injuries and avoid hazards, adolescents should be well trained and supervised. Former secretary of labor Robert B. Reich and the Department of Labor launched a public education campaign in 1996 called "Work Safe This Summer" to help teen workers avoid tragedy and educate employers on safety precautions.

Less enforcement

No laws are effective without adequate enforcement. Budget cuts starting in the Reagan administration in the early 1980s reduced the investigative staff at the Labor Department and OSHA. Many states have also tightened their enforcement budgets. In 1996, just 815 federal investigators monitored all labor violations, down from over 1,000 in the early 1980s; in general, investigators respond only to complaints. More funds for labor law enforcement require support from Congress.

To encourage employers to obey the laws, Congress raised the civil penalties for child labor violations from $1,000 to $10,000 in 1990. In 1994, the Labor Department set a fine of up to $10,000 for each violation leading to the serious injury or death of a child.

Attempts to change the laws

For the most part, child labor laws strike a balance between protecting young workers from harm, providing them with rights on the job, and allowing employers to run their businesses. Yet employers have sought to change labor laws they consider overly restrictive.

Under pressure from supermarkets and other retailers, Congress revised the child labor laws in 1996 to allow teenagers to load materials into, but not operate, paper balers that meet federal safety standards. Teenagers under age eighteen had been prohibited from loading and operating the heavy machines used to crush and bind cardboard boxes, as many minors working with paper balers had been injured in the past. A seventeen-year-old worker in Pennsylvania was killed when he reached into a baler to free some jammed paper, according to the Child Labor Coalition, which opposed the change.

Also in 1996, a bill was introduced in Congress to allow sixteen- and seventeen-year-olds to drive on the job, if driving is not the primary duty of their employment. Under cur-

A California official investigates a garment industry sweatshop that employs children. Enforcement of child labor laws is hindered by budget cuts and reduced staff.

rent law, they are only allowed to drive on the job in an emergency. Representative Randy Tate (R-Washington) sponsored the bill after fifty-nine auto dealerships in his state were fined for allowing teenage employees to drive. The florist industry also supports the bill, which is still pending.

In rare cases, child labor laws go beyond what the government intended. In 1993 Tommy McCoy, a fourteen-year-old batboy for the Class A Savannah Cardinals baseball team, was fired after a Labor Department official told the team it was violating labor laws when he worked past 7 P.M. on school nights and 9 P.M. during the summer. "The application of child labor laws in the case of fourteen-year-old batboys does, at first glance, look silly," responded Labor Secretary Reich. "It is not the intent of the law to deny young teenagers employment opportunities as long as their health and well-being are not impaired." Batboys were granted an exemption from the law in 1996.

National efforts are under way to improve child labor laws. The Young American Workers Bill of Rights was introduced in Congress in the early 1990s. The bill would provide more resources for enforcing child labor laws and stiffen the penalties for violators. New limits on the hours a sixteen- and seventeen-year-old can work during the school year would be set; and the work certificate system would be strengthened to ensure that jobs are legal and safe. Also, children and parents would be better informed about a young person's rights and protections in the workplace. The bill was still under consideration by Congress in 1997.

Being aware of labor laws

Unlike young people in many countries, young Americans have strong health and safety protections in the workplace. By knowing the labor laws, minors on the job can avoid being exploited by employers who ask them to work too many hours or at dangerous tasks. If an employer asks a fifteen-year-old to drive a motor vehicle or work more than three hours on a school day, the teenager should know that this is against the law.

6

When Children Break the Law

JUST AS IN the workplace, children accused of breaking the law have historically been given special protections. The juvenile justice system was established one hundred years ago to help troubled children. Rather than punishing children who commit crimes, the juvenile courts were designed to rehabilitate youths to leave their troubled pasts behind and become law-abiding adults.

But the rehabilitative aims of juvenile justice came under criticism in the 1990s after the nation saw a sharp rise in juvenile crime. From 1986 to 1995, the numbers of juveniles arrested for violent crimes rose by 67 percent—and for murder by 90 percent. Teenagers with easy access to guns and drugs and a seemingly casual attitude towards violence appeared to be a growing menace. Was the juvenile justice mandate to help delinquent youths failing to protect society?

Many people blamed the juvenile justice system for being ineffective and too lenient, and questioned the special rights and protections it provides even to violent offenders. Critics began demanding harsher penalties for juveniles and a lower age at which juveniles who commit certain serious crimes are charged, tried, and sentenced in the adult criminal justice system.

In response, states are processing an increasing number of violent juveniles in the adult criminal justice system. Today a fourteen-year-old charged with robbery in the first degree in New York State is tried as an adult in supe-

rior court, not in family or juvenile court, and, if found guilty, he or she will have a criminal record.

Juvenile justice at work

Just like an adult criminal defendant, the fourteen-year-old will face a jury in the New York's supreme court. But he or she will be sentenced as a "youthful offender," which means a more lenient sentence than an adult would receive. Also, the teen will be incarcerated in a secure facility operated by the state Division for Youth, not an adult prison, at least until the age of sixteen.

In many important ways, juveniles are treated differently than adults. These differences stem from the fundamental philosophy of juvenile justice, which is a civil system aimed at changing children's behavior, not branding them as criminals.

Juvenile offenders—who are under eighteen in thirty-nine states, seventeen in eight states, and sixteen in three states—fall into two categories: delinquents who break a criminal law and status offenders who break a law that applies only to juveniles, such as running away from home, repeatedly disobeying their parents, or truancy. Status offenses would not be crimes if an adult committed them. Many states handle status offenses in the social services systems.

In 1995 there were an estimated 2.7 million arrests of persons under age eighteen, or 18 percent of all arrests, according to the U.S. Department of Justice. Arrests of juveniles accounted for 9 percent of murders, 15 percent of forced rapes, 20 percent of robberies, and 13 percent of aggravated assaults that were cleared by arrests. Juveniles under age fifteen were responsible for 30 percent of juvenile violent crime arrests. However, the majority of youths do not break the law: less than one-half of 1 percent of all persons ages ten through seventeen were arrested for a violent crime in 1995.

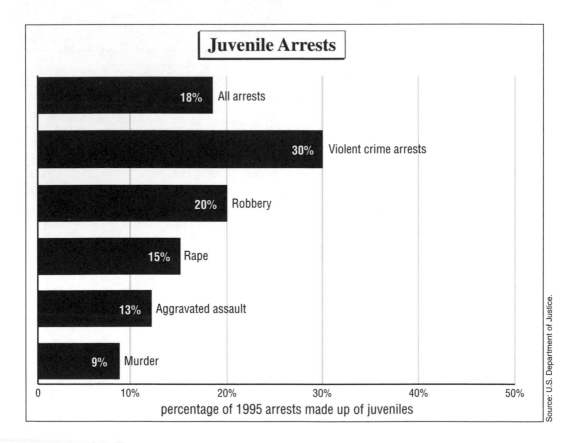

Juvenile Arrests

18% All arrests

30% Violent crime arrests

20% Robbery

15% Rape

13% Aggravated assault

9% Murder

0   10%   20%   30%   40%   50%

percentage of 1995 arrests made up of juveniles

Source: U.S. Department of Justice.

When a teenager is taken into custody

Generally, a teenager taken into custody for breaking a law is brought to a police station for booking. Parents or guardians are contacted, and the juvenile is sent home or held in a secure detention center until a court date. Unlike adults, minors do not have the right to post bail, which would allow them to be released until their court date. However, juveniles must have a pretrial detention hearing within twenty-four hours to determine whether they should be held in a juvenile detention center or allowed to go home.

Juveniles who are arrested today have significantly more legal rights than they did thirty years ago. Until the 1960s, minors were not entitled to most of the basic procedural protections spelled out in the Bill of Rights, such as the right to a lawyer and due process.

One of the first cases to turn the tide was that of a troubled sixteen-year-old named Morris Kent. In 1961, Kent confessed to police in the District of Columbia that he broke into a woman's apartment, raped her, and took her wallet. As a juvenile, he had no right to a hearing to

Police search a group of teenagers for weapons. Because they are young, juvenile offenders are viewed as less culpable than adults.

determine whether the case would be heard in juvenile or adult criminal court, where the punishment would be more severe. Ignoring requests from his lawyer for a hearing, the juvenile judge moved the case to criminal court. Kent was found guilty of housebreaking and robbery and sentenced to thirty to ninety years in prison.

The Supreme Court in *Kent v. U.S.* (1966) found the boy had not been granted due process of law when the case was moved to adult court without a hearing. Due process, guaranteed by the Fifth Amendment, protects persons accused of crimes from unchecked justice with the promise that certain specific procedures will be followed. The Court found that Kent was treated as an adult criminal, yet his constitutional right to due process was ignored because he was a juvenile. "There is evidence, in fact, that there may be grounds for concern that the child receives the worst of both worlds: that he gets neither the protections accorded to adults nor the solicitous care and regenerative treatment postulated for children," wrote Justice Abe Fortas.

Rights for arrested minors

More landmark Court decisions about juvenile rights were to follow *Kent*. One of the most important cases was *In Re Gault* (1967), which began when a fifteen-year-old Arizona boy was taken into custody along with a friend for making an obscene phone call. His parents were not notified of his arrest, nor was he advised of his right to have a lawyer or the right to remain silent. The juvenile court judge committed him to a state industrial school until age twenty-one, and the case was appealed to the Supreme Court.

The Court found that juveniles are entitled to certain rights following an arrest, including the right to a lawyer, the right to early written notification of the charge, the right against self-incrimination, the right to confront and cross-examine their accuser, and the right to remain silent. Another high court ruling gave minors the right to the "proof beyond a reasonable doubt" required in criminal court to establish guilt. By the end of the 1960s, youths accused of crimes were guaranteed many of the rights of adults.

Juvenile court

Yet youths in juvenile court still do not have certain rights, including, in most states, a jury trial or a public hearing. These differences reflect the notion that delinquents should not be judged publicly by society, but instead rehabilitated by professionals experienced in helping troubled youths, and given the chance to reform and enter adulthood with a clean slate.

In 1992 the nation's juvenile courts handled 1.5 million delinquency cases, or four thousand each day, according to the U.S. Department of Justice. In about one-third of the cases, the juvenile court judge decides informally whether to dismiss the charges or place the child on probation or in an alternative program, like drug counseling or a curfew. These cases usually involve minor infractions, which do not warrant the child's removal from home. Otherwise, the youths are sent to juvenile court for an adjudicatory hearing, a nonjury trial before a juvenile court judge.

The court's actions and confidentiality

The judge uses the hearing to determine whether the youth broke the law. The youth has a right to a lawyer, who will speak on his or her behalf. The judge may also hear testimony from the arresting officer, crime victim, and other witnesses. If a law was broken, then the youth is determined to be a delinquent, and a ward of the state. This differs from criminal court, where the offender would be formally convicted and sentenced. The distinctive language points again to the belief that a child is not as culpable as an adult, but rather needs help and guidance.

The court then examines the youth's background, and the judge issues a disposition, which might include probation, fines, community service, or placement in a foster home, training school, or other secure setting. The judge may also recommend education, drug and alcohol counseling, or job training. Youths may be placed on probation or in confinement until they reach a certain age, which is seventeen in most states. States will extend this time limit for serious cases, eventually transferring the youth to an adult facility.

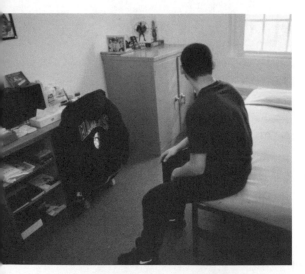

Only a small percentage of juvenile offenders are held in secure facilities, such as this one. Some people view this as evidence of excessive leniency in the juvenile justice system.

Since confidentiality is important in the juvenile justice system, reporters and spectators are not allowed in juvenile court. Juvenile court records are private, although thirty states allow limited access with a court order. But public outrage over juvenile crime has pushed some states to release information about juveniles involved in serious crimes or chronic offenders.

Getting tough with juveniles

The perception of an epidemic of violent teenagers is fueled by news reports of teenagers committing brutal, senseless crimes. In 1997, a fifteen-year-old girl, the adoptive daughter of wealthy parents and a student at a Jesuit school on New York's Upper West Side, was arrested, along with a fifteen-year-old boy, for stabbing a forty-four-year-old man to death in Central Park one night and dumping his body in a lake. The three had been drinking beer together. At the time of the teens' arrest no reason was given for the murder, according to news reports.

This case and others like it have provoked a mixture of public outrage and fear. The worst of the teenage crimes have led people to wonder how to prevent irrational and ruthless behavior by teenagers. "A 14-year-old with a gun in his hand is far more menacing than an adult because a teenager will pull the trigger without fully considering the consequences. He'll pull the trigger over a leather jacket, a pair of sneakers or a joke," criminologist James Alan Fox of Northeastern University told *Newsweek*. These teenagers, he said, show "absolutely no respect for human life."

Some people feel the juvenile system is too lenient with violent juveniles. The two teenagers in New York will be tried as adults on a charge of second-degree murder, but New York law protects them from the severity of adult sentences. Recent figures show just 9 percent of juveniles found to have broken the law are incarcerated; instead, most are put on probation.

In an effort to get tough with young offenders, states are making it easier for juveniles to be tried as adults in criminal court, where sanctions are more severe. Since 1978, at least forty-four states have decreased the age or added new offenses for transferring juveniles to criminal court.

Every state now allows youths who commit certain serious crimes and chronic offenders to be tried in criminal court. A case can be transferred to criminal court in three ways: the seriousness of the crime excludes it from juvenile court; the prosecutor requests the case be moved; or the juvenile judge decides the case should be heard in criminal court. Murder, armed robbery, and rape will send a juvenile as young as thirteen years old to criminal court in some states.

The numbers of juvenile delinquency cases transferred to criminal court increased from 7,000 in 1988 to 11,700 in 1992. In 1995, about 3 percent of juveniles arrested were sent to adult criminal court, according to the U.S. Department of Justice. Many of these youths will wind up in adult prisons, although current federal and state laws require them to be separated from adult prisoners. As of 1997, some 6,500 youths younger than eighteen were in state prisons and jails across the country.

Should teenagers be tried as adults?

Not everyone agrees that treating juveniles like adults is the best way to stem juvenile crime. At least two recent studies have shown that defendants tried in adult courts were more likely to be arrested again than those kept in the juvenile system, writes Anthony Lewis in the *New York Times*.

In addition, some people feel that a thirteen- or fourteen-year-old is not competent to stand trial as an adult. "Children don't stop being children just because they commit a crime," said Judge William Hibbler, of the Cook County Juvenile Court, in the *New York Times*. Critics also worry that police and prosecutors will not distinguish between the hardened teenage criminal and the adolescent who made a mistake and would be better served in the juvenile system.

Indeed, some people contend that adult prisons are dangerous for young inmates. Children in adult prisons are more likely to be sexually assaulted, physically abused, and attacked with weapons than juveniles in youth facilities, reports the American Civil Liberties Union. "Many juveniles tried as adults are housed in correctional facilities with adults where they are denied access to treatment, education, and vocational training, and are exposed to a more hardened and experienced group of offenders," states N. Lee Cooper, president of the American Bar Association.

In a ruling that may influence the debate, the Indiana Court of Appeals decided in May 1997 that a teenage girl, Donna Ratliff, should not be imprisoned with adults. Donna was abused and molested by family members as a child. When she was fourteen, she set fire to her house, and her mother and older sister died in the fire.

Because the crime was serious, she was tried as an adult. Donna was found guilty of manslaughter and sentenced to twenty-five years in Indiana's maximum security prison for women. But after serving eighteen months of her sentence, the court ruled that imprisoning Donna with adults violated the state constitution, which requires that Indiana has separate institutions for "correcting and reforming juvenile offenders" and to keep them apart from hardened adult criminals. The ruling meant Indiana would have to move eighty-five other inmates under age eighteen from state prisons to juvenile facilities.

But the American public appears to support tougher treatment for juveniles. In 1997 Congress was preparing to pass a major federal juvenile crime bill removing many of the protections of the juvenile justice system. The legislation, supported by President Bill Clinton, would provide federal funds to states that try more young people in adult court, and ease the rules that juveniles and adults be kept apart in prison. Teenagers under a certain age who commit federal felonies would be subject to trial in federal court.

Juveniles and the death penalty

A youth tried as an adult is subject to adult sentences, including the death penalty. In March 1997, fifty-eight persons were on death row because of crimes committed at age sixteen or seventeen, or about 2 percent of the total death row population of 3,122, according to Victor Streib, dean of the Ohio Northern University Pettit College of Law and an expert on the topic.

Juveniles convicted of murder have been sentenced to die since the colonial era, but from 1948 until the late 1980s no execution of persons under sixteen took place, reflecting public distaste for putting children to death. As Supreme Court Justice John Paul Stevens stated in a 1988 decision regarding the death penalty for juveniles: "The imposition of the death penalty on a fifteen-year-old offender is now generally abhorrent to the conscience of the community."

Historically, states set the minimum age for the death penalty, without federal guidelines. Some states allowed

Supreme Court justice John Paul Stevens ruled that juveniles who are under sixteen at the time of their offense cannot be sentenced to death.

children as young as ten or twelve to be sentenced to death. Then in 1988, the Supreme Court considered the case of a fifteen-year-old convicted of first-degree murder and sentenced to death. In *Thompson v. Oklahoma*, the justices ruled that the "cruel and unusual punishment" prohibition in the Eighth Amendment of the Constitution does not allow the execution of a person under sixteen at the time of his or her offense.

Justice Stevens stated in the decision that a juvenile is not as culpable for a crime as an adult because "inexperience, less education, and less intelligence make the teenager less able to evaluate the consequences of his or her conduct while at the same time he or she is much more apt to be motivated by mere emotion or peer pressure than is an adult."

A year later, the Court decided in *Stanford v. Kentucky* (1989) that the Eighth Amendment does not prohibit the death penalty for crimes committed at ages sixteen or seventeen. Thus, the Court was clear: sixteen- or seventeen-year-olds can be sentenced to death. Today, in the thirty-eight states that allow capital punishment, the minimum age for the death sentence is seventeen in four states, sixteen in twenty-one states, and eighteen in thirteen states.

Nine persons convicted as juveniles have been executed since the Supreme Court ruled the death penalty was constitutional in 1976, according to Streib. While the number of death row inmates has increased by 165 percent from 1983 to 1997, from 1,209 to 3,200, the number of juveniles with death sentences has fluctuated but remained "fairly constant," according to Streib.

One of those executed was Christopher Burger, who was seventeen and a soldier at Fort Stewart, Georgia, when he and another soldier murdered a cab driver. Burger was convicted in 1978. His attorney, Andrea Young, tried unsuccessfully to commute the sentence to life in prison, arguing that Burger was brutally abused as a child, then abandoned by his parents. After Young and anti–death penalty advocates exhausted all appeals, in 1993, at age thirty-three, Burger was executed for the crime he committed as a minor.

Support and opposition

The majority of Americans support the death penalty. In addition to preventing murderers from killing again, many proponents say murderers give up their right to live when they take someone else's life.

Those who oppose capital punishment say it is immoral to kill a person, no matter how brutal the crime. They assert the death penalty discriminates against the poor and minorities, especially defendants who cannot hire their own attorneys. They point out that some people sentenced to death have later been found innocent. And they cite studies that show the death penalty does not deter violent crime.

Death penalty opponents are particularly against imposing the sentence on juveniles, contending that a sixteen- or seventeen-year-old is not mature enough to take full responsibility for his or her actions and face the ultimate punishment. More than seventy countries that allow the death penalty have banned it for offenders under age eighteen, and many international human rights standards prohibit such executions, including the United States Convention on the Rights of the Child. "They are not adults. They have not had the experience of adults," says Watt Espy, director of the Capital Punishment Research Project. "A lot of parents need to be punished instead of the kids."

Demonstrators show their support for the death penalty. Most Americans support the death penalty, but opinions are more divided on whether it is moral to execute minors.

How far will the nation go?

The death penalty for juveniles is likely to get more attention as states look for ways to stem juvenile crime. But just how far the nation will go to overhaul the juvenile justice system—and remove the traditional rights and protections granted to children in trouble —remains to be seen.

Some advocates say stiffer sentences will not address the roots of juvenile crime, such as poverty, substance abuse, and broken families, and call for more innovative solutions. "States that have experimented with community programs for delinquent youth have shown success in reducing crime," states Vincent Schiraldi, director of the Justice Policy Institute in Washington, D.C., in a letter to the *New York Times*. In Boston, a program of prevention, intervention, and enforcement for violent young offenders reduced youth homicides by 80 percent over five years. More funding for the juvenile court system is also needed. A study by the Children and Family Justice Center of the Northwestern University School of Law found that the juvenile court in Cook County, Illinois, is so overburdened that about 70 percent of cases are dismissed for lack of evidence because prosecutors do not have the resources to research the evidence, leaving the juvenile free to go without the help he or she may need.

Yet there are positive signs. In 1995, juvenile arrests for violent crime fell for the first time in almost a decade, and the decrease was greatest among younger adolescents.

"Their voices will be heard"

In the courts and elsewhere, the rights of children in the United States are constantly evolving. No longer are children considered mere possessions of their parents, as they were in the Colonial era, but rather as full citizens with many of the legal rights of adults. Howard Davidson, director of the American Bar Association's Center on Children and the Law, told *Newsweek* a few years ago, "It's far more likely today that children will be treated with respect and dignity, and that their voices will be heard."

Yet children are not adults, and sometimes they need special protection, particularly in difficult times. "Everywhere we look, children are under assault: from violence and neglect, from the breakup of families, from the temptations of alcohol, tobacco, sex and drug abuse, from greed material-ism, and spiritual emptiness. These problems are not new, but in our time they have skyrocketed," wrote Hillary Rod-ham Clinton in *It Takes a Village*.

Still, when school officials or legislators attempt to shield children from harm or control their behavior with school safety programs or teenage curfews, they must not ignore their legal rights and liberties. In 1943, the Supreme Court decided in the landmark case *West Virginia v. Bar-nette* that students in public schools are not compelled to salute the flag. Public schools must act within the limits of the Bill of Rights, wrote Justice Robert H. Jackson: "That they are educating the young for citizenship is reason for scrupulous protection of Constitutional freedoms of the in-dividual, if we are not to strangle the free mind at its source and teach youth to discount the important principles of our government as mere platitudes." His words still hold true today, not just in the schools, but in all parts of Ameri-can society where young people are active participants.

Organizations
to Contact

The following organizations are concerned with children's rights. They address issues from family planning to juvenile justice, preventing child abuse to protecting First Amendment rights for student journalists.

Alan Guttmacher Institute
120 Wall St., 21st Fl.
New York, NY 10005
(212) 248-1111

The institute promotes family planning and sex education programs through its well-respected research, public education, and policy analysis work.

American Bar Association Center on
Children and the Law
740 15th St. NW
Washington, DC 20005-1009
(202) 662-1720
http://www.abanet.org/child

Founded in 1978 by the ABA Young Lawyers Division, the center's mission is to improve the quality of life for children through law, justice, and public policy. The organization provides information on child abuse and neglect, foster care, termination of parental rights, child custody, parental kidnapping, and related issues.

American Civil Liberties Union (ACLU)
132 W. 43rd St.
New York, NY 10036
(212) 549-2500
http://www.aclu.org

The ACLU is a nonprofit, 275,000-member public interest group, with affiliates in all fifty states, devoted to protecting the civil liberties of Americans and extending them to groups that have traditionally been denied them. Through lobbying and litigation, the ACLU works to assure that the Bill of Rights is preserved. The ACLU sponsors national projects devoted to children's rights, education reform, reproductive freedom, and workplace rights.

American Humane Association (AHA)
Children's Division
63 Inverness Dr. East
Englewood, CO 80112-5117
(303) 792-9900
http://www.sni.net/aha/cpmain.htm

The AHA, founded in 1878, is a national association of child welfare professionals, educators, researchers, judicial and law enforcement professionals, and child advocates. The association, through its Children's Division, advocates improved services for children and families at risk of abuse and neglect.

American Library Association
Office for Intellectual Freedom
50 E. Huron St.
Chicago, IL 60611
(800) 545-2433
http://www.ala.org

The association's Office for Intellectual Freedom works to educate libraries and the general public about the importance of intellectual freedom in libraries. The office publishes the monthly *Intellectual Freedom Action News* and the *Banned Books Week Resource Guide,* with information on books that have been challenged.

Child Help USA
National Child Abuse Hotline
(800) 422-4453

This national hotline, staffed by professionals, handles calls from people in crisis and provides referrals in all counties across the United States. The hotline is a resource for legal assistance, advocacy, treatment programs, shelters, and more.

Child Labor Coalition

National Consumers League
1701 K St. NW, Suite 1200
Washington, DC 20006
(202) 835-3323

The coalition, as part of the National Consumers League, advocates safe working conditions for young workers and promotes improved child labor laws and programs to reduce the hazards for minors in the labor force.

Children's Defense Fund (CDF)

25 E St. NW
Washington, DC 20001
(202) 628-8787
http://www.childrensdefense.org

The national organization researches and lobbies for programs and policies affecting children, particularly those who are poor or minority. Founded by Marion Wright Edelman, a leader in children's rights, CDF works on issues including children's health, welfare, development, poverty, employment, and violence.

Child Welfare League of America (CWLA)

440 First St. NW, 3rd Fl.
Washington, DC 20001-2085
(202) 638-2952
http://www.cwla.org

A national nonprofit membership organization of over eight hundred child welfare agencies serving over 2 million children and their families, CWLA, established in 1920 to protect abused and neglected children, is a recognized leader in advocacy for children in crisis.

National Center for Juvenile Justice

710 Fifth Ave., Suite 3000
Pittsburgh, PA 15219
(412) 227-6950
http://www.ncjj.org

The Research Division of the National Council of Juvenile and Family Court Judges works to prevent delinquency, child abuse, and neglect through research and distribution of information on issues relating to juvenile justice.

National Committee to Prevent Child Abuse
332 S. Michigan Ave., Suite 1600
Chicago, IL 60604-4357
(312) 663-3520
http://www.childabuse.org

Founded in 1972, the committee consists of volunteers who work with local and national groups to prevent child abuse through public service campaigns, prevention programs, and public policy. The committee publishes a variety of educational materials on parenting, child abuse, and child abuse prevention.

Planned Parenthood Federation of America
810 Seventh Ave.
New York, NY 10019
(212) 541-7800
http://www.igc.apc.org/ppfa/welcome.html

Planned Parenthood is an international organization promoting reproductive health care and family planning. Through its nine hundred health centers nationwide, Planned Parenthood offers contraceptive information and services, testing and treatment for sexually transmitted diseases, pregnancy testing, and other services.

Student Press Law Center
1101 Wilson Blvd., Suite 1910
Arlington, VA 22209-2248
(703) 807-1904
http://www.splc.org

The center is a nonprofit organization devoted to protecting the First Amendment rights of high school and college journalists. A national legal aid agency, the center provides legal assistance and information to students and faculty advisers experiencing censorship or limits to a free student press.

Suggestions for Further Reading

Tricia Andryszewski, *Abortion: Rights, Options, and Choices.* Brookfield, CT: Millbrook Press, 1996.

Janet Bode and Stan Mack, *Hard Time: A Real Life Look at Juvenile Crime and Violence.* New York: Delacorte Press, 1996.

Nancy Day, *Violence in Schools: Learning in Fear.* Springfield, NJ: Enslow, 1996.

Leah Farish, *Tinker v. Des Moines: Student Protest.* Springfield, NJ: Enslow, 1997.

John C. Gold, *Board of Education v. Pico (1982).* New York: Twenty-First Century Books, Henry Holt, 1994.

Ted Gottfried, *Privacy: Individual Right v. Social Needs.* Brookfield, CT: Millbrook Press, 1994.

Laura Offenhartz Greene, *Child Labor: Then and Now.* New York: Franklin Watts, 1992.

Kathleen A. Hempelman, *Teen Legal Rights: A Guide for the '90s.* Westport, CT: Greenwood Press, 1994.

Andy Hjelmeland, *Kids in Jail.* Minneapolis: Lerner, 1992.

Margaret O. Hyde, *Kids in and out of Trouble.* New York: Cobblehill Books, 1995.

Elaine Landau, *Child Abuse: An American Epidemic.* Englewood Cliffs, NJ: Julian Messner, 1990.

Marianne LeVert, *AIDS: A Handbook for the Future.* Brookfield, CT: Millbrook Press, 1996.

Milton Meltzer, *Cheap Raw Material: How Our Youngest Workers Are Exploited and Abused.* New York: Viking, 1994.

David E. Newton, *Teen Violence: Out of Control.* Springfield, NJ: Enslow, 1995.

Ross R. Olney and Patricia J. Olney, *Up Against the Law: Your Legal Rights as a Minor.* New York: E. P. Dutton, 1985.

Elaine Pascoe, *Freedom of Expression: The Right to Speak Out in America.* Brookfield, CT: Millbrook Press, 1992.

Peter Sgroi, *Blue Jeans and Black Robes: Teenagers and the Supreme Court.* New York: Julian Messner, 1979.

Ryan White and Ann Marie Cunningham, *Ryan White: My Own Story.* New York: Dial Books, 1991.

Youth Communication, *The Heart Knows Something Different: Teenage Voices from the Foster Care System.* Ed. Al Desetta. New York: Persea Books, 1996.

Works Consulted

"The Adolescent's Right to Confidential Care When Considering Abortion," *Pediatrics*, vol. 97, no. 5, May 1996.

"Adoption for Foster Children," *New York Times* editorial, May 8, 1997.

AIDS Policy Center at George Washington University, *Changing Faces, Changing Directions: State Responses to the Demographic Shifts in the HIV/AIDS Epidemic*. Washington, DC: George Washington University Press, May 1995.

Alan Guttmacher Institute, *Lawmakers Grapple with Parents' Role in Teen Access to Reproductive Health Care*. New York: Alan Guttmacher Institute, 1995.

Alan Guttmacher Institute, *Teenage Reproductive Health in the United States*. New York: Alan Guttmacher Institute, 1994.

Clara Bingham, "The Child-Labor Sting," *Newsweek*, March 26, 1990.

Briefings of the Commission on Security and Cooperation in Europe, *Migrant Farmworkers in the United States*. Washington, DC: U.S. Government Printing Office, May 1993.

Herbert Buchsbaum et al., "The Law in Your Life," *Scholastic Update*, September 17, 1993.

Fox Butterfield, "Few Options or Safeguards in a City's Juvenile Courts," *New York Times*, July 22, 1997.

Fox Butterfield, "Indiana Court Bars Mixing of Young and Adult Inmates," *New York Times*, May 15, 1997.

Fox Butterfield, "With Juvenile Courts in Chaos, Some Propose Scrapping Them," *New York Times*, July 21, 1997.

Dawn N. Castillo, *Preventing Deaths and Injuries of Adolescent Workers*. Cincinnati, OH: National Institute for Occupational Safety and Health, 1995.

Child Labor: Increases in Detected Child Labor Violations Throughout the United States. Washington, DC: U.S. General Accounting Office, April 1990.

William Claiborne, "Judge Strikes Some California Immigrant Bans," *Washington Post*, November 21, 1995.

Rebecca Clark et al., *Fiscal Impacts of Undocumented Aliens: Selected Estimates for Seven States*. Washington, DC: Urban Institute, 1994.

Thomas Condon and Patricia Wolff, *School Rights: A Parent's Legal Handbook and Action Guide*. New York: Macmillan, 1996.

Coordinating Council on Juvenile Justice and Delinquency Prevention, *Combating Violence and Delinquency: The National Juvenile Justice Action Plan*. Washington, DC: U.S. Department of Justice, 1995.

Conna Craig and Derek Herbert, *Languishing in Foster Care*. Washington, DC: National Center for Policy Analysis, 1997.

John DiConsiglio and Karen N. Peart, "Closing the Golden Door," *Scholastic Update*, November 15, 1996.

Margaret Dornfeld, *The Turning Tide: From the Desegregation of the Armed Forces to the Montgomery Bus Boycott (1948–1956)*. New York: Chelsea House, 1995.

William Dowell, "Her Dying Prayers," *Time*, May 5, 1997.

Brian Dumaine, "Illegal Child Labor Comes Back," *Fortune*, April 5, 1993.

John Ellement, "SJC to Review School Condom Plan," *Boston Globe*, March 6, 1995.

John Ellement, "State High Court OK's Falmouth Plan to Provide Condoms in Public Schools," *Boston Globe*, July 18, 1995.

Haya El Nasser, "More Schools Test Kids for Drugs," *USA Today*, September 5, 1996.

Jon Engellenner and Denny Walsh, "Suit Won't Halt Drug-Sniffing Dogs for Now," *Sacramento Bee*, March 23, 1997.

Abigail English et al., *State Minor Consent Statutes: A Summary*. San Francisco: National Center for Youth Law, 1995.

Louie Estrada, "Loudon School Must Mainstream Autistic Boy," *Washington Post*, December 5, 1996.

Barri R. Flowers, *The Adolescent Criminal: An Examination of Today's Juvenile Offender*. Jefferson, NC: McFarland, 1990.

James Alan Fox, "The Calm Before the Juvenile Crime Storm?" *Population Today*, September 1996.

Caroline Fraser, "Suffering Children and the Christian Science Church," *Atlantic Monthly*, April 1995.

Freedom Forum First Amendment Center, *Death by Cheeseburger: High School Journalism in the 1990s and Beyond*. Arlington, VA: Freedom Forum First Amendment Center, 1994.

Ted Gest and Victoria Pope, "Crime Time Bomb," *U.S. News & World Report*, March 25, 1996.

Tim Golden, "Abortion Law Is Overturned in California," *New York Times*, August 6, 1997.

Tim Golden, "Before the Dance, a Sobriety Check," *New York Times*, February 10, 1997.

Abby Goodnough, "Internet Access Puts Burden of Control on Schools," *New York Times*, April 19, 1997.

Abby Goodnough, "New Jersey's School Financing Is Again Held Unconstitutional," *New York Times*, May 15, 1997.

Ellen Greenberger and Laurence Steinberg, *When Teenagers Work: The Psychological and Social Costs of Adolescent Employment*. New York: Basic Books, 1986.

Kathleen A. Hempelman, *Teen Legal Rights: A Guide for the '90s.* Westport, CT: Greenwood Press, 1994.

Marguerite Holloway, "Hard Times: Occupational Injuries Among Children Are Increasing," *Scientific American*, October 1993.

Sari Horitz, "In D.C. Schools, Security Is Getting Personal," *Washington Post*, April 25, 1994.

John Hubner and Jill Wolfson, *Somebody Else's Children: The Courts, the Kids, and the Struggle to Save America's Troubled Families*. New York: Crown, 1996.

Human Rights Watch, *United States: A World Leader in Executing Juveniles*. New York: Human Rights Watch, 1995.

Michele Ingrassia and John McCormick, "Why Leave Children with Bad Parents?" *Newsweek*, April 25, 1994.

"Juvenile Injustice," *America*, September 28, 1996.

Juvenile Justice: Juveniles Processed in Criminal Court and Case Dispositions. Washington, DC: U.S. General Accounting Office, 1995.

Ken Kay, "More Cities Consider a Curfew for Teens," *Fort Lauderdale Sun-Sentinel*, September 8, 1996.

Louise Kiernan, "Kids Wait Years for Fresh Starts," *Chicago Tribune*, February 9, 1997.

Gwen Kinkead, "Chinatown-I," *New Yorker*, June 10, 1991.

Jonathan Kozol, *Savage Inequalities: Children in America's Schools*. New York: Crown, 1991.

Mary Beth Lane, "Defense of School Vouchers Pledged," *Cleveland Plain Dealer*, January 11, 1996.

Tamar Lewin, "Parental Consent to Abortion: How Enforcement Can Vary," *New York Times*, May 28, 1992.

Anthony Lewis, "Crime and Politics," *New York Times*, May 19, 1997.

Anthony Lewis, "Suffer the Children," *New York Times*, July 7, 1997.

"Little Progress on Child Abuse," *New York Times* editorial, August 17, 1997.

Michael Martinez, "'Dark Side' of Internet Worries School Officials," *Chicago Tribune*, October 5, 1995.

John McCormick, "How a Dedicated Judge Bucked the System by Putting Children First," *Chicago Tribune*, March 24, 1997.

Stephen McFarland, "City's Litany of Death and Disgrace," *New York Daily News*, March 31, 1997.

Ken McLaughlin et al., "Judge Guts Core of Prop. 187," *San Jose Mercury News*, November 21, 1995.

Tom Morganthau, "The Lull Before the Storm," *Newsweek*, December 4, 1995.

National Abortion and Reproductive Rights Action League, *Restrictions on Minors' Access to Abortion*. Washington, DC: National Abortion and Reproductive Rights Action League, April 1997.

National Child Labor Committee, *Child Labor in the '90's: How Far Have We Come*. Washington, DC: National Child Labor Committee, 1994.

National Consumers Action League and the Child Labor Coalition, *Child Labor Monitor*. Washington, DC: National Consumers Action League, June 1996.

National Institute of Corrections Information Center, *Offenders Under Age 18 in State Correctional Systems: A National Picture*. Longmont, CO: U.S. Department of Justice, 1995.

Ron Nixon, "Caution Children at Work," *Progressive*, August 1996.

Gary Orfield et al., *Deepening Segregation in American Public Schools*. Cambridge, MA: Harvard Graduate School of Education, 1997.

People for the American Way, *Attacks on the Freedom to Learn*. Washington, DC: People for the American Way, 1996.

"Playing Politics with Adoption," *New York Times* editorial, June 10, 1997.

Janet R. Price, Alan H. Levine, and Eve Cary, *The Rights of Students: The Basic ACLU Guide to a Student's Rights.* 3rd ed. Carbondale: Southern Illinois University Press, 1988.

Amy Pyle, "L.A. School Board Gets Plan to Re-Integrate Disabled Students," *Los Angeles Times*, December 17, 1996.

Reproductive Freedom Project of the American Civil Liberties Union, *No Way Out: Young, Pregnant, and Trapped by the Law*. New York: Reproductive Freedom Project of the American Civil Liberties Union, 1991.

Lynda Richardson, "Progress on AIDS Brings Movement for Less Secrecy," *New York Times*, August 21, 1997.

Dale Russakoff, "The Protector," *New Yorker*, April 21, 1997.

Cintra Scott, "Censored," *Seventeen*, June 1995.

Howard N. Snyder, *Juvenile Arrests, 1995*. Washington, DC: Office of Juvenile Justice and Delinquency Prevention, 1997.

Howard N. Snyder and Melissa Sickmund, *Juvenile Offenders and Victims: A National Report*. Washington, DC: Office of Juvenile Justice and Delinquency Prevention, 1995.

David Stoesz and Howard Jacob Karger, "Suffer the Children," *Washington Monthly*, June 1, 1996.

Rachel L. Swarns, "Agency Was Warned About Foster Mother Charged in Girl's Death," *New York Times*, July 2, 1997.

"Teen Curfews," *Issues and Controversies on File*, Facts On File News Services, 1996.

Index

Picture Credits

About the Author

Ann Malaspina is a writer who specializes in urban, social, and children's issues. She was born in Brooklyn, New York, and grew up in Connecticut and Georgia. She earned a B.A. in English from Kenyon College and an M.S. in journalism from Boston University. Ms. Malaspina worked as a features writer and reporter for newspapers in Massachusetts before moving to New York, where she freelances for newspapers, magazines, and reference publishers. She lives in Jackson Heights, New York, with her husband, Robert Harold, an attorney with the Legal Aid Society, and their sons, Sam and Nicholas.